Evangelizing Immigrants

Outreach and Ministry Among Immigrants and their Children

Glenn Rogers

Published by
Mission and Ministry Resources

www.missionandministryresources.net

Table of Contents

Acknowledgements

Many people have helped make this book a reality and they deserve mention and thanks. First is my wife, Glenda, who encouraged me to write it and assisted in conducting the interviews. Then there are the missionaries who introduced me to leaders of immigrant churches: Mike Landon and Larry Henderson. The ethnic church leaders who assisted us by inviting us to their churches to conduct our interviews were also very helpful. These include: Henry Roncancio, Oscar Mejia, Sixto Rivera, Carlos Acosta, Sovanna Tim, Edward Leung and Bob Lo. To all of these brothers in Christ, a sincere *Thank You*, and may the Lord continue to bless you in your work in his kingdom.

Finally, to the fifty believers who agreed to share their stories with us and give us the advice we asked for, to each one, *Thank You* and may the Lord bless you as you live to serve him.

Introduction

Before leaving this earth to ascend back to the Father, Jesus commissioned his followers to go and make disciples of all the nations (Matthew 28:18-19). The Greek phrase for *all the nations* is *panta ta éthnē,* which could also be translated *all ethnic groups.* The story of what God has done for humanity through the life, death and resurrection of Jesus is to be told among every ethnic group in the world. The sacrifice has been for all people. The story is to be told to all people.

Challenges

Over the centuries, the church has tried to be faithful in carrying out the Great Commission. Missionaries have traversed the earth to tell the story of Jesus. Many people have heard the story and responded, accepting God's offer of mercy and grace. But there are still many people who have yet to hear the story of Jesus told in a culturally appropriate way. From a missions perspective, there is still a lot of work to do. Global population stands at 6.5 billion. Of those 6.5 billon, 2.1 billion identify themselves as Christians (Barrett, Johnson, Crossing 2006). A good number of the 4 plus billion people who are not Christians are Muslims. Many are Hindus. Many of them have no religion at all. Most Chinese, for example, are simply non-religious. Those 4 billion people, whether they have existing religious affiliations or not, need to hear about God's offer of grace and mercy through Jesus Christ. There is still a lot of mission work to be done.

One of the challenges of telling the story of Jesus to the 4 billion people who are not yet Christians is that in many of the countries where those people live Christian missionaries are not welcome. In many places, Satan has made it extremely difficult for Jesus' followers to tell his story. Even in countries where a missionary presence is not illegal, living in those countries as a missionary presents many challenges, so many in fact, that those taking up the call to foreign missions has dropped dramatically. Fewer Christians are making long-term commitments to foreign missions. There is not only a lot of work to be done, it is getting harder to do and fewer believers are stepping up volunteering to go.

Opportunities

God is always at work in his world, creating opportunities for his people to do what he has asked them to do. At this point in history an amazing thing is happening: people from all over the world are immigrating to America in astonishing numbers. People from nearly every culture on the planet are pouring into the United States at rates that are unprecedented in recent history. And while some people see the present level of immigration creating serious social and economic challenges, should not God's people see this as an opportunity?

At present, there are 193 countries recognized as sovereign nations. In any given decade that number may change by two or three in either direction as geopolitical regions are reapportioned. But for the foreseeable future humankind is likely to remain divided into fewer than 200 countries. However, there are nearly 7,000 cultures in the world. There are 6,912 recognized language groups. Each language group constitutes a separate culture. But some cultural groups share the same language even though they are separate cultures. For instance, there are 22 cultures that utilize the Spanish language. So there are more cultures than there are language groups.

There are fewer than 200 countries, but nearly 7,000 cultures in the world. Many countries (in the geopolitical sense) are home to more than one cultural group. For instance, Nigeria, West Africa, is home to nearly 250 different cultural groups. China's population represents over 52 different linguistic and cultural groups.

Some of those 6,912 language groups are small indigenous groups of people in developing world countries and do not represent a major world population group. Statistically they are lumped into one of the 193 countries that make up our present global community. Regardless of how those people are grouped statistically, the crucial factor for the Christian community to recognize is that people from nearly all of those 193 countries have immigrated to America. The Dallas Independent School District, for instance, reports that almost 70 different languages are spoken in the homes of the children enrolled there (www.dallasisd.org). In population centers such as New York and Los Angeles those numbers would be even higher.

Immigration

The people of the world have come to America. And they have come not only to major population centers such as New York, Los Angeles, Miami, Chicago, and Dallas/Fort Worth, they have come to every State in our nation. Granted, some geographic regions have larger immigrant populations than do others, but an immigrant population is present in each of our fifty states. People from far away places, with cultural perspectives very different from our own have come to our communities, towns and cities. They live and work among us. And many of them do not know Jesus. They do not understand Christianity. Should Christians not see this as an amazing opportunity the Lord has given us?

The church still needs to think in terms of foreign missions. Both human and financial resources are needed to be faithful to Jesus' command to go and make disciples. God's people must cross geographic and cultural boundaries to tell the story of Jesus to people who will live out their lives in those far away places. We cannot ease up on foreign missions. However, since millions of people each year are coming to the United States from those far away places, the church needs to put significant resources (both human and financial) into cross-cultural missions right here in North America. We need to tell the story of Jesus to those who have immigrated to America. We need to plant ethnic churches all across our great nation.

Purpose

This book is not about the sociopolitical issue of legal and/or illegal immigration to the United States. The heated debates over immigration issues and the political rhetoric designed to appeal to voters has no place in this study. This book is about effective evangelism primarily among first generation immigrants to America. Secondarily it has to do with outreach to successive generations of immigrants not yet fully assimilated into mainstream society. Regardless of one's political convictions and loyalties, if one is a Christian, evangelism among immigrants ought to be a primary concern.

My purpose in this study is to assist church leaders in thinking about the opportunity that exists for outreach among immigrants, and to discuss methods of effective outreach. What is the best way to accomplish this purpose? First, I believe we need to spend some time considering some statistics about immigration and think about what is involved in the process of immigration. If we want to reach immigrants with the Good News about Jesus, we must understand immigrants: who they are, why they come, and the struggles they have in adjusting to a new culture.

Second, if we want to reach immigrants with the Good News about Jesus, we need to understand how to do that effectively. Where would one go to get that kind of information? To immigrants who have already been converted.

The foundation for this presentation is the data that was gathered during a series of interviews with 50 first generation immigrants from seven different cultures regarding their conversion experience. The interviews were conducted in the Dallas-Fort Worth Metroplex in 2006. An interview guide (reproduced in Appendix A) was used in each interview to guide the process, assuring uniformity throughout the research project.

Interviews with six immigrant ministers, four Latino and two Asian, who lead ethnic churches also inform this study. Their observations about ministry among immigrants and their advice to church leaders who want to reach out to immigrant communities is insightful and helpful. The interview guide used in those interviews is included in Appendix B.

Scope

Every research project must have boundaries. The boundaries of this study have to do with:

1. who was interviewed: first generation immigrants from several different religious backgrounds (Catholicism, Buddhism, Daoism/Taoism, and a number of people who

were non-religious) who were converted to a conservative Protestant form of Christianity after arriving in America,

2. where they were interviewed: in the Dallas-Fort Worth Metroplex between April and June of 2006,

3. the number of interviews conducted: 50,

4. the numbers of cultures the interviewees represented: seven—Mainland China, Cambodia, Laos, Taiwan, Mexico, Honduras, Colombia.

Because of the limited scope of this study there are issues that cannot be addressed. For instance, since this research has to do with first generation immigrants, issues involving generations 1.5 or 2 are not primary concerns. This is not to suggest that issues related to generations 1.5 and 2 are not important. They are. They are simply beyond the scope of this study.

Definitions

In the context of this study the following terms will be used in the ways described:

1. *Immigrant*: Someone who is not born in this country who comes to live in this country. The term should not be considered negative or derogatory in any way. It is simply a term that designates a person who leaves his or her home culture and moves to another culture. The term foreign-born is sometimes used as a synonym for immigrant.

2. *First Generation Immigrant*: Someone who is an adult when they leave their home culture to immigrate to a new country.

3. *Generation 1.5*: Someone who is not an adult when they immigrate (usually with their parents) to a new culture. This is somewhat of a *fuzzy* concept. Obviously someone who is seventeen when he or she immigrates is not yet an adult (by American standards) but is more of an adult than a child and

would most likely be considered a first generation immigrant. A child, however, from infancy to early teens, should be counted as a generation 1.5. The distinction between generation 1 and 1.5 is important because it is easier for a child to learn and adapt to the new culture than it is for an adult. The older the immigrant, the harder the acculturation and assimilation processes are. That is why, for research purposes, immigrant children have their own immigration category: generation 1.5.

4. *Generation 2*: The American-born children of generation 1 or 1.5s—children born after immigration has occurred.

5. *Enculturation*: The process of learning one's own culture as a child.

6. *Acculturation*: The process of learning a second culture later in life.

7. *Assimilation*: The intentional process of engaging in a new culture, becoming part of the mainstream of the new society one has adopted.

8. *Religious Conversion*: When I refer to the *religious conversion* of the immigrants we interviewed I am referring to the change in their religious beliefs and status that occurred as they changed from being either: 1) a non-religious person, 2) a non-Christian person, or 3) a Catholic Christian to become a conservative Protestant Christian. This is not to suggest that a conservative protestant expression of Christianity is the only acceptable expression of Christian faith. Rather, conversion to a conservative protestant form of Christianity is simply the context and frame of reference of this specific study.

9. *Latinos*: Immigrants from Spanish speaking cultures. There is a debate as to proper terminology. People with a Mexican ancestry prefer the term Hispanic. People from South American cultures prefer Latino. There are also Caribbean Spanish speaking cultures: Cuba, Puerto Rico, and the Dominican Republic. In government documents, such as census material, the term Hispanic seems to be the

designation of choice. However, in academic circles, the term Latino appears to be preferable. To simplify matters, I have chosen to use the term Latino when referring to peoples from Spanish speaking cultures.

10. *Anglos*: White people—even though many white people are not actually members of the Anglo-Saxon ethnic group.

11. *Ethnic Churches*: churches made up of ethnic groups other than Anglos.

Assumptions

My assumptions for this study are:

1. that the most accurate and valid source of information on the reasons immigrants are converted will come from the immigrants who have been converted,

2. that those who were converted after immigrating to America would be willing to discuss their conversion experience, explaining what led to their conversion, that is, what influences were present that motivated them to embrace their new faith,

3. that their conversion experiences would be very similar (insofar as *why* they were converted) whether they had those experiences in California, Texas, New York, Florida, Illinois or some other North American geographic region,

4. and that it was, therefore, not necessary to travel to different regions of the country to conduct interviews.

Methodology

A one-page interview guide was developed to lend consistent structure to the interview process. The interviews were conducted in a personal one-on-one setting. My wife, Glenda, assisted me in this research conducting a number of the interviews.

It was not my intention to gather and present quantifiable data, but rather qualitative data that could be presented in narrative form, enabling the individuals to speak for themselves, telling us how and why they were converted.

Overview

In Chapter 1 we will spend some time looking at immigration statistics and patterns in an attempt to understand the realities of our multiethnic American society. Chapter 2 will focus on the challenges of immigration, including acculturation and assimilation. Chapter 3 will be a presentation of the data gathered from the individuals we interviewed.

In Chapter 4, I will provide an analysis of the interview profile data and make some observations regarding what we learned. In Chapter 5, I will present information gathered from a number of ministers (who are themselves immigrants) who work with either Latino or Asian immigrants. They will discuss the challenges of their work and the methods they use in outreach and ministry. They will also offer some advice to church leaders who are thinking about beginning outreach among a specific immigrant group.

Chapter 6 will be a brief overview of the processes involved in planting ethnic churches. Chapter 7 will be a brief discussion about the missional church in a multiethnic society.

The basic question is, how can churches increase the effectiveness of their outreach among immigrants? That's what this book is about.

What You Won't Find

What you won't find in this book is an outline for a program of immigrant evangelism or a magic formula for planting and growing an ethnic church. Have you ever wondered why Jesus commissioned his followers to go and make disciples among all ethnic groups but didn't tell them how to do it? The reason Jesus didn't reveal to his followers a program of outreach or a sure fire church planting method is that there is no such thing. There is no program or method of outreach that works with all people in all cultural contexts. It would be nice if there was, but there isn't. So this book does not contain programs or formulas.

What this book does contain is perspective and information that you need to develop ways of working effectively among the immigrants that have come to your community. If you are wise and if you ask for the Lord's help he will bless you. With his blessing and with the help of the people who speak through this book you will find avenues of effective ministry to your immigrant community.

Chapter 1

The World Is Coming To America

In June of 2002, the National Center for Policy Analysis ran an article in Daily Policy Digest with a headline that read *Rate of Immigration to the U.S. Highest in 150 Years* (NCPA 2002). The article went on to note that more immigrants are coming to America than at any time since the 1850s. The 2000 census revealed that there were, at that time, 31.3 million people who were not born in the U.S. making their home here. That amounted to 11.3 million more foreign-born residents than had been counted in the 1990 census. In 2000, immigrants made up 11.1 percent of our total population: 51.7 percent of those immigrants were from Latin American countries, 26.4 percent were from Asian countries, 15.8 percent were from Europe, 2.8 percent were from Africa, 2.7 from Canada, and 0.5 percent were from Oceania.

In a discussion of the impact immigration will have on Christianity in America in the coming years, Philip Jenkins notes:

> As the nation grows, its ethnic character will also become less European and less White, with all that implies for religion and cultural patterns. For most of American history, the racial

15

question essentially concerned two groups, Black and White, people of African and European descent. In 1930 the nation was comprised of 110 million Whites, 12 million Blacks, and just 600,000 "Others," meaning Native Americans and Asians. From the 1960s on, the Otherness of America developed apace, largely due to a relaxation of immigration controls. As we gain greater distance from the event, the passage of the Immigration Reform Act in 1965 increasingly looks like the most significant single event of that much-ballyhooed decade. By 2000, the United States was home to 30 million immigrants, about 11 percent of the population. Over 13 million migrants arrived in the 1990s alone. Almost 5 percent of Americans have been in the country for a decade or less.

American society is steadily moving from a Black and White affair to a multicolored reality. In 2000, 35 million Americans were counted as Hispanic, almost 60 percent of them of Mexican ancestry. Nearly 12 million more Americans were Asian, of Chinese, Japanese, Filipinos, Vietnamese, and Korean stock. Asians and Hispanics combined make up 15 percent of the population today, but this share is projected to grow to almost 25 percent by 2025, and to 33 percent by 2050 (2002:100).

As the ethnic makeup of our society changes, so does the ethnic makeup of the church—or at least it should. If we are doing our job, it will.

Immigration Patterns and Statistics

In 2003, the population of the United States included 33.5 million people who were not born in the U.S. That is 11.7 percent of the total population: 53.3 percent of those foreign-born residents were from Latin American countries, 25 percent were from Asia, 13.7 percent were from Europe, with 8 percent coming from other countries. Two-thirds of immigrants from Latin American countries were from Mexico (Larsen 2004).

16

Countries of Origin

Of all the legal immigrants who arrived in the U.S. in the fiscal year of 2003 (that is, between October 1, 2002 and September 30, 2003), over half were from only ten countries:

116,000	Mexico
50,000	India
45,000	Philippines
41,000	China
28,000	El Salvador
26,000	Dominican Republic
22,000	Vietnam
15,000	Cambodia
14,000	Guatemala
14,000	Russia (Meyers and Yau 2004).

As noted above, the majority of immigrants are of Latino and Asian origin.

Regions of Settlement

Where are all of these immigrants going when they arrive in the U.S.? There are six states in the U.S. which seem to attract most of the immigrants: California, New York, Texas, Florida, New Jersey, and Illinois (Meyers and Yau). According to Larsen, in 2003, 11.3 percent of immigrants lived in the Midwest, 22.2 percent lived in the Northeast, 29.2 percent living in the South, and 37.3 percent of immigrant lived in the West. In fact, 38.6 percent of all Latin American immigrants live in the West, as do 44.5 percent of Asian-born immigrants (2004).

Additionally, also according to Larsen, in 2003 44.4 percent of foreign-born residents lived in an urban context rather than a rural culture. U.S. cities with the largest immigrant populations (in 2000) include: Los Angeles, New York, San Francisco, Miami, and Chicago (Census Bureau 2002: CENBR/01-1).

It must not be assumed, however, that immigration and immigrant population does not impact every state of our nation. In 1990, to say nothing of 2006, every state in the U.S. had an immigrant population (Wright 2002:299).

Latino Immigrants

In 1960, about nine percent of the immigrant population was comprised of Latino peoples. By 1990, the number had increased to 44 percent. The main countries of origin for Latino immigrants included: Cuba, Dominican Republic, El Salvador, and Mexico. By 2000, immigrants from Mexico accounted for more than 25 percent of all immigrants in the U.S. and more than half of the total of Spanish speaking immigrants. Most of them live in Southern California and Texas (Census Bureau 2002: CENBR/01-2).

Many people who immigrate to the United States eventually become naturalized citizens. Only 28 percent of Latino immigrants become U.S. citizens, while 52 percent of immigrants from Europe and 47 percent of immigrants from Asian countries become U.S. citizens. Since the majority of Spanish speaking immigrants are from Mexico, it becomes obvious that Mexican attitudes towards U.S. citizenship have a significant impact on the percentage of Latinos becoming citizens. Reasons for this will be discussed in more detail in my discussion of assimilation (Census Bureau 2002: CENBR/01-2).

Of all Spanish speaking immigrants over 25 years old, 50 percent of them had a high school education or higher when they immigrated to the U.S. However, 80 percent of those with a high school education or higher were from South American cultures. Only 34 percent of Mexicans had a high school education or higher (Census Bureau 2002: CENBR/01-2).

Occupationally, 12 percent of Spanish speaking immigrants were classified as professional or managerial with half of those being of Mexican descent. Seventy-one percent of all Latino immigrants were employed in skilled labor, service or farm labor jobs. Eighty-three percent of Mexican immigrants were employed in non-management or non-professional jobs (Census Bureau 2002: CENBR/01-2).

In 1999, the median annual income of individual immigrants from Spanish speaking countries was $21,000 for men and $17,200 for women. Median annual household income was $29,400 (Census Bureau 2002: CENBR/01-2). At the time of this writing (2006) it is likely that increases have occurred (though specific data is unavailable). The numbers, however, are alarmingly low and reflect the educational levels and occupational classification of many Latino immigrants.

The size of households among immigrants from South American cultures averaged 3.72 persons, compared to non-immigrant American households of 2.54 persons. By comparison, the households of immigrants from Mexico averaged 4.21 persons (Census Bureau 2002: CENBR/01-2).

Asian Immigrants

In 2000, 25 percent of America's foreign-born population came from Asian countries. This represents a steady increase. In 1970, the figure was nine percent; in 1980, it was 19 percent. Forty-five percent of the nation's Asian population can be found in three major metropolitan centers: Los Angeles, New York and San Francisco (Census Bureau 2002:CENBR/01-3). However, in a speech delivered in Addison, Texas, in 2004, Ambassador Sichan Siv, the United States Representative to the United Nations Economic and Social Council, noted that according to the U.S. Census Bureau, "Texas is one of the fastest growing states in terms of Asian population. It is also the third largest with Asian-owned businesses, totaling about 60, 200," (Siv 2004).

19

In 2000, a full 47 percent of immigrants from Asian countries had become naturalized U.S. citizens. Only immigrants from Europe have a higher rate of citizenship— 52 percent (Census Bureau 2002: CENBR/01-3). As noted earlier, only 28 percent of immigrants from Latino countries become citizens.

Eighty-four percent of Asian immigrants 25 years old or older had a high school education or higher. For the foreign-born population across the board, only 67 percent had an educational level of high school or higher (Census Bureau 2002: CENBR/01-3).

In 1999, Asian immigrant households enjoyed a median annual income of $51,400, compared to a median annual income of $36,000 for all other immigrant households. These numbers reflect the educational levels and occupational classifications (including business ownership) of Asian immigrants.

The average Asian household was comprised of 3.18 persons, compared to the average of all immigrant households of 3.26 persons per household (Census Bureau 2002: CENBR/01-3). The average is slightly higher than the average native-born American household of 2.54 persons, but lower than the average Latino number of 4.21 persons.

Immigration in 2004

In 2004, according to the Department of Homeland Security immigration statistics (2004:22), there were nearly 1 million legal immigrants admitted to the United States. Every state in the U.S. (and the District of Columbia) had immigrants who registered their intention to reside in that state. California had the largest number, 252,920, with New York second at 102,390. Wyoming had the fewest with 295. In 2004, only ten states added fewer than 2,000 new immigrants to its existing foreign-born population.

Department of Homeland Security immigration statistics:

Total Immigrants:	946,142
Genders:	
Men:	430,662
Women:	515,314
Married:	561,886
Ages:	
25-29	124,406
30-34	143,921
35-39	107,251
Under 1	7,807
Over 75	10,936
Occupation:	
Executive/managerial	31,689
Professional/technical	73,862
Service	38,566

Some Immigration Projections

Forecasting is not an exact science. What will happen in 10, 20 or 40 years from now depends on many factors, including whether immigration laws change or remain the same. As social scientists and statisticians examine trends of the past and present it is possible to suggest with some measure of accuracy what is likely to occur in the future if past and current trends remain steady.

If past and current immigration trends remain steady, what will the U.S. population look like in the coming years? "In less than 50 years, the U.S. Census Bureau projects that immigration will cause the population of the United States to increase from its present 288 million to more than 400 million," (Center for Immigration Studies). Those numbers represent an increase in U.S. population (by 2050) of 112 million directly attributable to foreign-born residents. Others suggest a more realistic number may be 80 million (Edmonston). However, when the U.S. Census Bureau projects a total U.S. population in 2050 of 419,854,000 (U.S. Census Bureau 2004), suggesting that 112,000,000 of those

21

can be directly attributed to immigration, given past and current immigration trends, the figures do not seem out of line.

The point, as far as this study is concerned, is that recent immigration activity has impacted our society and will continue to do so in the coming years. As Christians given the task of getting the story of Jesus to every ethnic or cultural group of people on the planet, immigration is a godsend, perhaps in the very literal sense of the word!

Unauthorized Immigrants

Unauthorized immigrants (also referred to as illegal immigrants or illegal aliens) make up a significant percentage of the U.S. population. The issue of unauthorized immigrants generates a great deal of emotional debate. It is not my purpose here to suggest that either side of the issue is right or wrong. I am not entering the existing debate about unauthorized immigration. What I am doing is reporting the facts and reminding Christians that people who are here, authorized or not, who do not yet know our Lord need to be reached with the Good News about Jesus. So as you read the following statistical information, regardless of your philosophical or political position regarding unauthorized immigration, you must remember that Christianity and the Gospel rise above *all* sociopolitical concerns and debates. As Christians, our job is to share the Good News with every person, regardless of their sociopolitical status.

The data in this section is taken from the 2005 report by the Pew Hispanic Center in Washington, D.C. entitled: *Unauthorized Migrants: Number and Characteristics,* by Jeffery Passel.

In 2004 there were 35.7 million foreign-born people living in the U.S.

11.3 million (32%) were naturalized citizens
10.4 million (29%) were legal permanent residents
 1.2 million (3%) were temporary legal residents
 2.5 million (7%) were refugee arrivals
10.3 million (29%) were unauthorized immigrants

Of those 10.3 million unauthorized immigrants:

5.9 million (57%) were from Mexico
2.5 million (24%) were from other Latin American cultures
1.0 million (9%) were from Asian cultures
0.6 million (6%) were from Europe and Canada
0.4 million (4%) were from Africa or other regions

Most of these unauthorized immigrants have arrived since 1995, with the largest percentages arriving between 1995 and 1999.

Unauthorized immigrants fall into two major categories: those with visas (legal, appropriate documentation) who have stayed beyond the expiration of their visas (designated as *overstays*), and those who entered the country clandestinely or without documentation and inspection (designated as *EWIs*—entries without inspection). It is estimated that between 25% to 40% of unauthorized immigrants are *overstays*.

A large percentage of unauthorized immigrants enter the U.S. from Mexico—between 400,000 and 485,000 annually. However, it is important to know that after a number of years most have achieved the status of legal residents.

Where do these people live? Passel reports:

[T]he unauthorized population lives in just eight states: California (24%), Texas (14%), Florida (9%), New York (7%), Arizona (5%), Illinois (4%), New Jersey (4%), and North Carolina (3%). The appearance of Arizona and North Carolina on this list highlights another recent trend. In the past, the foreign-born population, both legal and unauthorized, was highly concentrated. But, since the mid-1990s, the most rapid growth in the immigrant population in general and the unauthorized population in particular has taken place in new settlement areas where the foreign-born had previously been a relatively small presence, (2005:11).

Though not mentioned in the passage above, Tennessee, Georgia, Maryland, Massachusetts, Virginia, Colorado, and Washington also have substantial immigrant populations (between 200,000 and 250,000), the direct result of the recent immigrant population diversification described by Passel.

Of the 10.3 million unauthorized immigrants in the U.S. (as of 2004), 81% of them were from Latin American cultures (Mexico, and Central and South America). But other than that broad characteristic (which tells us little) who are these immigrants? What are they like?

For the most part, they are members of a family or household, they are relatively young, and all of the adults in the family work. Typically, they are not highly educated, they earn low incomes, there is a high rate of poverty among them and they do not enjoy the benefits of health insurance.

The 10.3 million unauthorized immigrants in the U.S. live in 6.3 million families that total 13.9 million people. The difference between the 10.3 and the 13.9 is the number of U.S. born children (over 3 million) that are part of the unauthorized immigrant families. Generally speaking, unauthorized immigrant families are younger, with 84% of those families consisting of adults between 18-44 years, compared to families of legal immigrants at 63% for that age category and non-immigrant families at 60% for that age range.

24

Educationally, a high percentage of unauthorized immigrant adults (between 25 and 64 years old) have lower educational levels than most non-immigrants. It must be noted, however, that in Mexico education is only required to the eighth grade. Thus, among unauthorized immigrant adults, 32% have less than a ninth grade education; 17% have completed education between the ninth and twelfth grades, and 24% have graduated from high school; 10% have completed some college, and 15% have earned a Bachelor's degree or more.

What kind of work do they do? Six broad occupational categories attract most unauthorized immigrant workers: farming, cleaning, construction, food preparation, production/manufacturing, and transport. The list below represents a number of occupational categories that do not include criteria for educational levels or licensure. The percentages indicate the percentage of unauthorized immigrants that make up the workforce in that occupational category:

Drywall/ceiling tile installers 27%
Cement masons & finishers 22%
Roofers 21%
Construction laborers 20%
Painters, construction etc. 20%
Brick/block/stone masons 19%
Carpenters 12%
Grounds maint. workers 26%
Misc. agricultural workers 23%
Hand packers & packagers 22%
Graders & sorters, ag. prod. 22%
Butchers/ meat, poultry wrkrs 25%
Dishwashers 24%
Cooks 18%
Dining & cafeteria attendants 14%
Food prep. workers 13%
Janitors & bldg cleaners 12%
Maids & housekeepers 22%
Sewing machine operators 18%

Cleaning/washing equip. oper 20%
Packaging/filling mach. oper. 17%
Metal/plastic workers, other 13%   (Passel 2005:27)

When stepping back from specific occupations to take a broader view of industry statistics, there are 11 industries where the number of unauthorized immigrant workers is more than twice that of the rest of the work force:

Landscaping services 26%
Private households 14%
Animal slaughter & process. 20%
Traveler accommodation 14%
Services to bldgs & homes 19%
Restaurants & food services 11%
Dry cleaning & laundry 17%
Construction 10%
Cut & sew apparel mfg 16%
Groceries & related prod 8%
Crop production 16%   (Passel 2005:29)

As one would expect given the educational levels of most unauthorized immigrants and the industries in which they work, income levels are lower for unauthorized immigrant families than for legal immigrant or non-immigrant families. Average family income for non-immigrant and legal immigrant families are nearly identical: $47,700 for non-immigrant families, and $47,800 for legal immigrant families. Average family income for unauthorized immigrants is only $27,400—about 43% lower.

As a result, "unauthorized immigrants are more than twice as likely to be living in poverty than native adults." Fewer than half of unauthorized adult immigrants have any form of health insurance. Some of their children do because of various state children's health insurance programs (Passel 2005:34-35).

Unauthorized immigrants are here and they are probably here to stay. In imagining Jesus being approached by a person who needed his attention, I find it difficult to imagine Jesus pausing to inquire as to the person's authorized or unauthorized social or legal status. Jesus didn't care about a person's social or legal status. And when it comes to helping those who need help, neither should we.

Summary

Latinos from all Spanish speaking cultures make up the largest group of foreign-born people living in the U.S. Asians from various cultures are the next largest group. Every state in the U.S. has an immigrant population and according to all projections and estimates the foreign-born population of the U.S. will continue to grow at impressive rates well into the middle of this new century.

People from other cultures are here and they are going to continue coming. Their presence is an opportunity for believers to tell the story of Jesus to people who may not have heard it before. Their presence here also provides us with an opportunity to demonstrate our Christian love and concern by living out our faith in meaningful ways as we reach out to our new neighbors to welcome, to help and to serve.

Unauthorized immigrants are part of the population mix and, like legal immigrants, are probably here to stay. Regardless of the various sociopolitical positions on "illegal immigration" that may be represented within the Christian community, as believers sent by our Lord to all ethnic groups, we should let the politicians hash out the sociopolitical issues. We should be busy reaching the immigrant population with the Gospel of grace.

Chapter 2

The Challenges of Immigration

People who have never immigrated to another country, especially one with a culture quite different from their own home culture, do not understand how traumatic the experience is. The familiar is replaced with the unfamiliar and an unsettling confusion that might be thought of as cultural sea-sickness overwhelms and destabilizes one's sense of being and well-being.

Imagine yourself driving at night into an unfamiliar neighborhood. You make a left turn and things begin to get weird. The street you were on before you turned disappears behind you and there's no way back where you came from. That's a little unsettling but you decide everything will be all right. In a while you notice that in this new neighborhood people not only drive on the other side of the street (the wrong side of the street!) but they do so upside down and backward, very fast! The houses in this odd neighborhood are floating just above the ground. Dogs are flying and birds are barking and you realize that you are not in Kansas anymore.

This Alice-in-Wonderland kind of madness is something like the cultural sea-sickness one experiences upon immigration to a new country with a new culture.

Why, then, would anyone want to immigrate to a new cultural context?

Why People Immigrate

America has always been a country of immigrants. That is our beginning, our history. Europeans came in droves to this new country. Roger Daniels observes that:

> The several hundred thousand Europeans who came to the New World in the sixteenth and seventeenth centuries came largely because of what we would now call the population and/or labor policies developed by the various colonizing powers. These policies were shaped both by the existing socioeconomic conditions in the home countries and by the opportunities for gain, real and imagined, that existed in the new colonies (2002:5).

In the beginning, people came to the New World looking for a new life, for opportunity, for freedom. Little has changed in nearly four hundred years.

Alejandro Portes and Ruben Rumbaut are straightforward in their response to the question, why do they come? "[T]oday's immigrants come because they can," (1990:8). They are speaking, of course, of legal immigration tied to the immigration act of 1965. Immigrants come to America because immigrants are welcome. But there is more to it than that. Why would people put themselves through the emotional trauma of immigration?

The American Immigration website lists seven reasons why people immigrate to America:

Political freedom
Religious tolerance
Economic opportunity—a better life, a better job
Political refugees fear for their lives
Some want a free atmosphere
Forced immigration
Family reunification   (American Immigration 2006)

Most of us are aware of the role religious freedom has played in the establishment and growth of our nation. Jon Butler and Harry Stout, in their Editor's Introduction to Jenna Joselit's book, *Immigration and American Religion,* discuss the relationship between immigration and religion.

> In America, the immigrant experience often has been the religious experience. From the 16th to the 21st centuries, immigrants have arrived in America fleeing religious persecution. Others found strength in religion as they faced a strange, enticing environment. Religion supported powerful institutions, secular and spiritual alike, that fostered immigrant ethnic identity. Everywhere religion shaped the immigrant social experience, from war and social reform to politics, family, and work.
>
> Immigrants created new churches, synagogues, and mosques. They adapted rituals and traditions to fit the style of a new land. They discovered new ways of thinking about religion, new ways of arguing about religion, and new ways of proclaiming religion. And their battles against religious prejudice gave the First Amendment's guarantees of religious freedom new life and renewed meaning. (2001:7).

Immigration and religion have always been connected. In their significant study entitled *Religion and the New Immigrants,* Helen Ebaugh and Janet Chafetz note that:

> The new immigrants, those who have arrived in the United States in the past three or four decades, have introduced diversity of all kinds into American society. They are racially and ethnically more varied than earlier streams of immigrants; they come from a greater variety of countries and continents; they speak more varied languages; and . . . bring with them religions that are either new or little known in this country, (2000:13).

It is certainly true that many immigrants bring their religions with them when they immigrate to this country. But many, for varying reasons, adopt a new faith after coming here. This is highly significant and merits our interest and inquiry.

Not all immigrants come to America for reasons related to religion. None of the immigrants we interviewed came to the U.S. for religious reasons. They came to America because of economic concerns, political concerns, or family concerns. Sometimes it was a combination of two or all three of those concerns. Many of the people we interviewed came to America with absolutely nothing. Some of them had lived in poverty before they came. They had nothing when they left their old county; they had nothing when they arrived in their new country—except hope. They hoped for a better life for themselves and their children.

Some immigrants, however, who arrived with next to nothing had left behind considerable assets. Some of the people we interviewed were highly educated professionals with successful careers in their home culture. One immigrant we interviewed from China had her Ph.D. in neuroscience and was an associate professor at a prestigious university. Her husband had been a successful architect. They had money, social status and security. Yet they walked away from it all and came to America with nothing to start over in a land of freedom and opportunity.

People who immigrate to America today do so for the same reasons people have always immigrated to this country: for the hope of a better life for themselves and their children in a land of freedom and opportunity. But many, upon arriving to take advantage of those freedoms and opportunities, also embrace Christianity. Understanding the context in which they make that decision is crucial.

Arriving In America

Most immigrants tell similar stories. The amount of paperwork and the time it takes to jump through all the immigration hoops to gain legal entry to this county can be

31

overwhelming. But that is not the focus here. The process is what it is and immigrants agree that living in this country is worth all the demands and procedures immigration requires. My purpose in this brief section is not to analyze the paper work end of the process, but to focus attention on the challenges of adjusting to a new life in a new culture.

Finding oneself in a new culture can be a very disorienting experience. If even language is not an issue, the challenges are formidable.

First (and these are not in order of importance or occurrence), there is the challenge of finding a place to live. Some immigrants to the U.S. arrive and join family already here. Living arrangements for those individuals may not be a challenge. But many immigrants arrive without the benefit of having extended family waiting for them. Temporary housing arrangements for a few weeks or a few months may have been arranged, but where in the vicinity of their point of arrival do they look for more permanent housing? What neighborhoods are desirable and which ought to be avoided? What is a fair price for rent? Then there are utilities: electric, gas, phone, and perhaps others. Each requires going to a different building or calling a different company. Deposits must be paid. How does one accomplish all these things without someone to help?

Second, there is getting settled and getting food and other necessary items so one can live. It's not like immigrants are on vacation. They can't spend money in restaurants, even fast food places are not practical for immigrants for more than a day or two, even if they have enough money for several days of McDonalds. In order to go shopping, immigrants have to get their currency exchanged and know how to use American money. They then have to know how to go shopping. Even such a simple task as grocery shopping can be overwhelming if one does not know how the system works. We assume that shopping is so easy that anyone could do it. You go into the store, walk down the aisle, select your items, put them in your cart, go to the checkout and put your items on the conveyer belt. The checker scans them, and tells you what the total is. You pay, you take your items and you go. What could be simpler?

It's not that easy. When my family moved to Nigeria to do mission work, we had an experienced couple take us under their wings to help us learn things like how to go shopping. In Nigeria the exchange rate usually hovered around 80:1. So to do shopping for staples—rice, beans, sugar, flour—things you normally bought in larger quantities, you had to carry thousands of naira (Nigerian money) with you. Then, when you went to the store, quite often there was no store—at least, not in the sense we normally think of a store. There was a market place where you haggled over the price with individual vendors. How much should three pounds of tomatoes cost in a Nigerian market?

On the occasions when there was an actual store to go into, buying simple things such as Q-Tips or band aids was a challenge because if you couldn't find them on the shelf and had to ask, no one understood what you were asking for. English is the official language of Nigeria, but it is British English spoken in Nigerian pidgin. When we asked for Q-Tips and band aids all we got were blank stares. In Nigeria band aids are called plasters (I still don't know why) and Q-tips, well, that's a brand name that they had never heard of. We had to describe what we wanted—small sticks with cotton twisted onto each end.

For a long time going shopping in Nigeria was either an adventure or a challenge because going shopping there is nothing like go shopping here. If we had not had another missionary couple to go with us and show us how things were done we might not have survived long in Nigeria.

It is important to remember that many of the immigrants who come to America come from cultures that are very different from ours. They have to learn how our money works, how to shop without bargaining over the price, how to choose which items to buy when there are twelve or twenty different kinds to choose from. In Nigeria, when we went to buy coffee, there was one kind. There was no choice. If you wanted coffee you bought what they had. Imagine being a Nigerian immigrant who wanted to buy coffee and going into a Walmart Superstore and finding the coffee aisle. How many brands of coffee would that Nigerian be confronted with: twenty perhaps? And then there is the difference between dark, medium or light roast. Should he or she buy ground coffee or beans that need to be ground? Should he buy regular or decaf? And what about all the designer options: hazelnut, vanilla, amaretto?

Multiply this coffee scenario 50 or 100 times (for all the other items one must buy to set up a household or do the weekly shopping) and it comes close to the kind of challenge and frustration an immigrant can experience in one simple task such as going shopping.

A third challenge immigrants face is transportation. If a vehicle can be purchased, then where one lives in relation to where one works is not as big of a concern. But what if there are no funds for a vehicle? Is there dependable public transportation? In some major cities, public transportation is affordable and readily available. In other places, the Southwest for instance, not having a car makes it difficult to do much of anything because everything is so spread out. In some regions, not having private transportation means having to live within walking distance of where one works. That factor may severely limit one's choice of accommodations, which impacts one's overall living conditions.

Fourth, immigrants with children have to be concerned with school. What schools will their children be going to? What grade levels will be appropriate for them? What about language and cultural concerns? The decision to

34

enter and live in a new culture has been made. That their children will learn a new culture is a given, but how will language and culture learning be handled? Matters that have to do with our children generate deep concerns. Concha Delgado-Gaitan and Henry Tureba address this issue in their book, *Crossing Cultural Borders: Education for Immigrant Families in America.*

A fifth major concern is language and communication. Have you ever tried to learn a second language? It's not easy, especially if you are an adult. The older a person is, the harder it is for him or her to learn another language. Much of a culture's nuances are contained in its language. The subtitles of how a people think are revealed in how they speak. Until immigrants are able to learn the language of their new culture, understanding and participating in that new culture in any meaningful way will be impossible. Earning a living can also be a challenge until the language barrier has been penetrated. All the tasks that are normally accomplished without much thought in one's daily routine present daunting challenges if a common language is unavailable.

I spent a week in Beijing, China, a couple of years ago, meeting with representatives of the Ministry of Education. Many of the high ranking officials spoke English. Most of the time I had the benefit of a business associate who was Chinese and spoke Mandarin. However, for several hours each day I was on my own. Breakfast was an adventure, as was shopping for a gift for my wife. At one point I had to negotiate a taxi by myself as well. How does one accomplish those simple tasks day-to-day without being able to communicate with the other people involved in the events? It can be a very frustrating experience, a frustration many immigrants put up with for an extended period of time until they can learn the language—which will be one of the hardest things they have ever done.

There are a number of other cultural concerns related, at least indirectly, to language learning and which can be challenging and frustrating. One of these is learning how to greet people. Some cultures bow, some embrace, some kiss, some shake hands. In some cultural contexts the exact ritual of greeting is highly significant. In Nigeria, for instance, part of the greeting ritual revolves around the precise time of day. It is important to know when to switch one's greeting from Good Morning, to Good Afternoon, to Good Day, to Good Evening. It is also crucial to know how long to engage in small talk before plunging into more serious matters. These may appear to be inconsequential concerns. But making repeated social blunders, even small ones, chips away at one's confidence and self-esteem, adding to existing pressures of culture adjustment.

Learning the new culture's perception of time can also be challenging. America is a very time conscious society. Productivity is linked to punctuality. Time is money. What many Americans fail to understand, however, is that our views regarding time are not shared by most of the people in the world. Most cultures are *event oriented* rather than time oriented. For most people in the world, being *in the moment with the people you are in that moment with* is more important than worrying about when the moment began, when it will end, and what will come after it ends. In other words, most of the world's cultures are more focused on relationship and person to person interaction than on the timeframe in which those events occur. In many cultures, events began when everyone important to the event arrives and once an event has begun it will continue until finished. When they are finished, the event ends and people move on to whatever is occurring next. In most cultures, the unfolding of the events is much more important than the timeframe in which the events occur. Only in Western society is the timeframe given priority over the event.

36

When immigrants from non-Western cultures come to America, one of the biggest adjustments they must make has to do with our obsession with the clock and punctuality. Because they are often "late" they are considered unorganized, undisciplined, rude, lazy or irresponsible. Most of the time, they are none of those things and are horrified to learn that their new fellow citizens think of them in those terms. They simply have a different set of priorities, a different view of what is important. Making the adjustment is difficult and takes a long time.

This discussion of cultural adjustment that immigrants must make could go one for many more pages but this should be sufficient to make the point: adjusting to a new culture, even one you chose to embrace, is a challenging, time-consuming, unsettling task that can turn one upside down and inside out. Learning a new culture as an adult is one of the most difficult challenges one can face in life.

Acculturation

Acculturation is the process of learning a second culture. It is a complicated, time consuming process. Understanding how we learn our primary culture as children (the process of *enculturation*) will provide some insight into the process of acculturation.

As children, we *absorb* our culture as it is *transmitted* to us more than we learn it in any intentional way as it is taught to us. As young people we are taught the grammatical rules of our language. Someone teaches us and we learn. It is an intentional process. Enculturation is a different process. Even before we are born we hear our parent's voices speaking the language that will become our own. As babies, we experience our world through sensory encounters: sights, sounds, smells, textures, tastes, and so forth that we do not fully comprehend. As toddlers we begin to explore,

37

to experience, to absorb. During our first few years of life, as we learn our language, we "learn" (unconsciously, and some better than others) the thought patterns and processes required to function in our culture. All the things we experience transmit to us something about the world in which we live in our given cultural context. As children, we do not analyze what we experience. For the most part, we simply absorb and accept it. Though many children go through a phase of asking "why," we accept most of what we "learn" (experience) without thinking about it.

Enculturation is, on our part, an unintentional act. Our parents, siblings and teachers intentionally instruct us, but seldom with the specific intent of teaching us our culture. That is why it is more accurate to speak of our culture being *transmitted* to us more than being *taught* to us. Think back to when your own children were young. Do you remember occasions when you specifically set out to teach them their culture? Probably not. Normally we do not think in those terms. However, when it comes to learning a second culture (acculturation), it is necessary to be intentional.

Children who immigrate (normally with their parents) at say eight or ten years old have been thoroughly enculturated in their home culture. They, like their parents, must now be acculturated, that is, they must learn a new culture. But because they are still children, they are still in what might be called an *active learning mode*. They still learn (and absorb) things quite easily. They will learn their new culture much more easily than their parents, who no longer learn as easily as they once did. Acculturation for young people (generation 1.5s) must be more intentional than their enculturation had been, but it will require less effort and less time than will be required for adults. Acculturation for adults (first generation immigrants) must be intentional and will be a slower process.

Surface-level Acculturation

In the simplest terms, culture learning occurs on two levels: the surface level and the deep level. It is possible, therefore to speak of *surface-level* acculturation and *deep-level* acculturation. Learning the surface-level features of a new culture is easier than learning the deep-level features. This is not to say that surface-level acculturation is easy. It is not. But compared to deep-level acculturation surface-level is *easier*.

What are the surface-level features of culture that immigrants must learn in the process of acculturation? To answer this question we must first think about what culture is and how it is constructed.

Paul Hiebert defines culture as *"the integrated system of learned patterns of behavior, ideas, and products characteristic of a society,"* (1983:25). Let's think about this definition. First, culture an *integrated whole*. It cannot be broken into individual parts. Different parts of culture can be analyzed and discussed, but as that which is "characteristic of a society" all parts of culture are interconnected. Second, culture is a *system*. The integrated parts work together to form a unified whole. Third, culture is *learned*, or as noted earlier, is transmitted and absorbed as children grow. Fourth, culture is *patterns of behaviors, ideas and products*. Culture is the way a people act, the way they think, the things they make. Culture is everything about a group of people.

We understand this part of culture. It is all the things we do and the way we do them as we go about our daily lives. But where does culture come from and how is it constructed? This is where things get a little complicated. I apologize for that, but it is necessary to grasp these ideas in order to understand how difficult acculturation is for people newly arrived in the U.S.

39

Culture is a three-tiered phenomenon made up 1) of our *deep-level* assumptions about the world and about how life is to be lived (called *worldview*), 2) of our *mid-level* internal values and our ways of feeling and thinking that grow out of our deep-level worldview assumptions, and 3) of our *surface-level* behaviors and structures. Figure 1 illustrates this three-tiered view of culture.

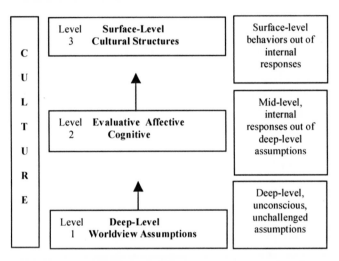

FIGURE 1: THREE-TIERED VIEW OF CULTURE

Think of culture as the house you live in. Our deep-level worldview assumptions about the world and how to live life serve as the foundation of your house. The house is then built on the foundation. Inside the walls of the building are the pipes, wires, conduit and ducting that make the house safe, comfortable and functional. The foundation and the stuff inside the walls remain mostly out of sight. What we think of as our house are the parts we see and touch: the exterior walls and interior partitioning, the parts that are, for all practical purposes, the house we live in.

Our deep-level worldview assumptions about life can be compared to the foundation of the house. Our internal values, feelings and thinking are the pipes and wires in the walls. The ways culture is lived out in everyday life is like the exterior and interior walls of the house. The foundation, pipes and wires are part of the house just as surely as are the walls, but because we don't see them we tend to forget them.

When you go to buy a house, the first thing you do when the real estate agent drives you up to the house, is look at the house—the outside of the house, the part visible from the street. When you go inside you take a quick look around to get a feel for the place. Then, if you are interested, you begin looking more closely.

The process of surface-level acculturation is like looking at the parts of the house that are visible, the parts easily seen and examined. We'll discuss looking at the wires and the foundation (deep-level acculturation) in the next section. For now let's focus on the details of surface-level acculturation.

Surface-level culture (level 3) is comprised of the behaviors and structures of a group of people. What kinds of things are these? Cultural structures are the frameworks we develop and use to accomplish the important activities of our society. Our educational system is a cultural structure, as is our political system. Our economic system (capitalism) is a cultural structure, as is our medical system. The various forms of religious expressions present in our society are cultural structures in that they allow us to express our faith in culturally appropriate ways. Our legal system is a cultural structure, as are our systems of transportation, our ways of structuring our families, our options for entertainment and recreation, our ways of celebrating or coping with the important events of life: births, weddings, deaths and so forth. These and other cultural structures allow us, as a cohesive society, to live out our lives in a meaningful, orderly, and for the most part, effective manner.

Cultural structures provide a framework for the way we do things (behaviors) as we live our lives. If our

41

educational system is a *cultural structure,* going to school is a *cultural behavior.* If democracy is one of our cultural structures, then voting is one of our cultural behaviors. Everything we do is a cultural behavior because all of our behaviors are carried out within the context of our culture. We do what we do the way our culture tells us to do it. We behave in culturally appropriate ways.

When we go out to eat in a restaurant, unless we are intending to enjoy a unique culturally-different experience, we sit on chairs and use silverware. To do so is, for us, culturally appropriate. In some cultures, going out to a restaurant would involve sitting on pillows on the floor and eating with one's right hand, primarily with the first and second fingers and the thumb.

Our cultural structures tell us what side of the road to drive on and when to stop and when to go. Our cultural structures tell us what parts of our bodies need to be covered in public, how to greet people, how to shop for the items we need for daily living, how to build our houses and how to arrange for sleeping and other activities in our houses. Our culture, through our unique set of linguistic symbols (including the rules for using those symbols) provides a means for communicating effectively with others who share our culture. Our culture provides a framework (guidelines) for appropriate behavior.

Surface-level cultural structures and behaviors (level 3 of our three-tiered cultural construct) are the ways we live out our ideas and assumptions about how life should be lived. These surface-level structures and behaviors are the first things people new to our culture must learn if they are to survive here.

Surface-level acculturation is not as simple as some might assume. Depending on what culture a group of immigrants might come from, our surface-level structures and behaviors might be very different from those of their home culture. Immigrants need to learn our cultural ways:

how to communicate, how to shop, how to send their children to school, how to take their children to the doctor, how to get a driver's license, how to find a place to live, how to have their utilities turned on, how to open a bank account, how to keep their immigration paperwork current, how to find a job, how to go to school. They need to learn about weddings and funerals, about voting and about going to the library, about getting along with neighbors, about hot dogs, apple pie and baseball, and about all the new opportunities that await them in this amazing place called America.

When immigrants face the very difficult challenge of learning a new set of cultural structures and behaviors, some friendly people to help explain and demonstrate can be very meaningful and deeply appreciated.

Deep-level Acculturation

As challenging as surface-level acculturation can be, deep-level acculturation is even more challenging. The reason for this is simple: surface-level acculturation involves learning the *what* and *how* of culture—what to do and how to do it. But deep-level acculturation involves learning the *why* of culture—why is American culture the way it is? Why do Americans think the way they think and behave the way they behave? Deep-level acculturation is about understanding the thinking and assumptions that result in surface-level cultural structures and behaviors.

For people new to American culture to understand why we are who we are, someone will have to be able to explain why we are the way we are. Finding someone who can do this is a challenge for immigrants because most Americans do not know enough history, philosophy and theology to know why we are the way we are. In all fairness, most cultural groups are like this. They know what they think and how they act—they know who they are. But they do not know why. Most cultural groups do not take the time

43

to figure out what their underlying worldview assumptions are.

Most Americans, for example, value their individuality. However, most Americans could not explain the historical or philosophical context in which our Western individualistic perspective developed. Most Americans know that we place a very high value on punctuality, but most of us could not explain the philosophical assumptions that underlie our near hypersensitivity to the issue. Most Americans appreciate direct, accurate communication even if it involves giving and receiving bad news or personal criticism, but most of us cannot explain the underlying assumptions that drive us to such brutal frankness.

This is why it is difficult for immigrants to understand the *why* of many of our cultural tendencies—no one seems to be able to explain the *why* to them. It would behoove church leaders to do some research not only into *who* we are as a people, but *why* so that we can assist immigrants in developing a deeper understanding and appreciation of our culture. It may also be that as we gain deeper insights into ourselves as a people that we may be better able to address some of our inadequacies.

How does one go about discovering his or her own deep-level worldview assumptions? There is no easy method, no shortcut. It requires a good deal of reading and thinking and it is beyond the scope of this small book to provide readers with the tools for that kind of introspection. Another of my books, *Understanding Anglo-American Culture: Why Are Anglos the Way They Are?* addresses that issue. My goal at this point is to give church leaders some idea of how difficult the acculturation process is.

Assimilation

Assimilation is the process of entering or becoming part of the mainstream, dominant culture of the society in which an immigrant has chosen to live (Thompson 1996: Vol. 1:112). Some social scientists lump acculturation and assimilation together as if they were not separate processes. But they are. It is entirely possible for an immigrant to achieve a high level of acculturation (culture learning) and yet resist the process of assimilation.

Being assimilated into another culture requires that the behaviors distinctive of one's home culture fade so deeply into the background (be repressed) that for all practical purposes they cease to function in any meaningful way. Assimilation requires a deep and fundamental change in both surface-level behaviors and deep-level assumptions that one's original cultural behaviors and assumptions cease to be factors in one's daily life. In other words, assimilation is a process of deep and fundamental change that changes a person from what they were into what they have now become.

Many immigrants (understandably) resist this kind of deep-level, pervasive change. They learn enough of our culture to be culturally functional, but they resist giving up who they are to (for all practical purposes) become someone else. Their reticence is understandable.

While some immigrants resist the process of assimilation, others embrace it. Some people come to the U.S. with every intention of being assimilated as quickly as possible. They want to become "Americans" in every sense of the word. Most people live between these two extremes, not resisting but not pursuing assimilation, allowing the process to occur naturally.

Assimilation will usually occur given enough time. If a first generation immigrant successfully resists assimilation, his or her children (whether generation 1.5 or generation 2) will be assimilated to some degree. By generation 3, complete assimilation is nearly inevitable. A family or sub-cultural group has to work very had to keep their children from being fully assimilated into mainstream society. Assimilation can be resisted but requires intentional effort.

The issue of assimilation can be confusing. Why would some people want to come to America but not want to become Americans? There are at least three good reasons.

First, just as we as Americans have a great deal of pride in our cultural heritage, people from other cultures have a great deal of pride in their cultural heritage. When my family and I lived in Nigeria, we did not want to stop being Americans. We were in Nigeria by choice. We loved the people and their culture had much to commend it. The Nigerian people we knew from a number of different tribes we happy, hard working people who loved their families and communities. They tried hard to be good people. We loved our Nigerian friends. But we were Americans and did not want to become Nigerians.

Second, most people enjoy a sense of personal identity that is linked, at least in part, to their group identity. Part of my personal identity includes the fact that I am an American. Many people from other cultural contexts link part of their personal identity to their cultural context as well. Even if they choose to live in a different cultural context, their personal identity remains linked to their home culture. They do not want to give up that part of their personal identity any more than most Americans would.

Third, the older a person is when they begin the acculturation process the harder it is to learn the deep-level part of a new culture. It is difficult to embrace a new value system and new patterns of thinking. For some people, those new values and new ways of thinking just never seem quite right. So they can never be fully embraced.

As Americans, we must accept the simple truth that as nice as we are, as rich and powerful as we are, not everybody wants to be us. People want freedom. People want opportunity. But they may not want to stop being who they are to become one of us. And that is perfectly acceptable.

Their Challenges Become Our Opportunities

Many immigrants arrive in America virtually empty handed. Some of them can't speak English. Some have no place to live, no job, no family. Some have all three and speak enough English to get by. But they don't understand the culture. Even with a basic support group in place (family, a job and a place to live) they will still experience a difficult period of culture shock that can lead to serious frustration and depression.

The challenges immigrants face as they adjust to a new life in a new culture become opportunities for God's people to make an important difference in the lives of people who need someone to make a difference in their lives during those difficult days. The challenges of immigration are open doors of opportunity for the church to step through and help people who need help.

Stepping through the door the Lord has opened for us may not be easy, but few worthwhile endeavors are. We need to begin seeing the challenges of immigration as opportunities to serve and make a difference in people's lives, just as Jesus did during his ministry.

Summary

People leave their home culture and move to a new country for many different reasons. Sometimes they are seeking religious freedom, sometimes freedom from political oppression. Often they are desirous of a better life. They want an opportunity to build something, to excel, to succeed. They want a better life for their children and grandchildren. So they come. They come to a new place. Some arrive with nothing but hope and anticipation. They are brave, determined people.

It is a wonderful place, America. But for those who come here from other cultures it is a strange place. It takes time to learn how to live here, to learn the surface-level cultural structures and behaviors. And it takes time to understand how Anglos think, to understand the deep-level assumptions about life that form Anglo values and ways of feeling and thinking.

And then, after becoming culturally functional, there is the whole assimilation issue—whether or not to let go of a big piece of oneself and become a different person. The challenges of immigration are enormous.

But with every challenge comes an opportunity. The challenge is theirs. The opportunity is ours. Can we step through the door the Lord has opened for us and make a difference in the lives of our new neighbors?

Chapter 3

Religious Conversion in the Immigration Process

This chapter will consist of a presentation of the data gathered in the 50 interviews conducted in the Dallas-Fort Worth Metroplex in 2006. The material is qualitative in nature and is presented in the random order in which the interviews occurred. There is a general cultural grouping (several people from Laos were interviewed one Sunday while several people from Cambodia were interviewed the following Sunday) but there is no intentional cultural grouping for presentation purposes.

A copy of the interview guide is included in Appendix A. The interview process was a simple one: after explaining our purposes to each interviewee and being granted permission to conduct the interview, we asked our interviewees the questions and recorded their answers in a simple straightforward manner. Their responses were then categorized into the three subdivisions of the profiles as they are presented below: background, conversion and advice.

Interview Profiles

1. Background: Meimei, is a 42 year old female from China who immigrated to America in 2003. She came to here join her husband who had been here as a student (working on a graduate degree at UTA). When her husband finished his degree program and got a job, Meimei came with their daughter to reunite their family. Meimei has a Bachelor's degree and in China was a journalist. Presently, she is studying to be a nurse.

Conversion: Meimei had been in America about 18 months before becoming a Christian. Meimei was attracted to the church because they offered free English lessons. She decided to take advantage of the opportunity not only as a way to improve her English skills but also to learn about American culture. Her English teacher was kind and helpful and Meimei wanted to understand these people who were being kind to her when they did not know her or seem to want anything from her. When asked why she had not become a Christian while in China, Meimei explained that "in China there is no God, no religion." Meimei (like most Chinese) sees America as a very religious country and she was impressed with the way Christians treated her. They were kind and helpful.

Advice: When asked what advice she would like to give church leaders about reaching out to immigrants, Meimei said churches should provide good language and culture teachers. They should not push for quick decisions and responses, but give immigrants time to understand. She also said that leaders must be friendly and open to new people and be willing to listen to concerns and questions and the feelings people will share with them. They must be willing to become friends with new people.

2. Background: Hua Wang is a 36 year old female from China who immigrated to America in 2001. Hua immigrated to America with her husband to find a job in her scientific field. Hua has a Ph.D. in neuroscience. Her specialty is research related to Alzheimer's disease. In China, Hua was an associate professor at a prestigious university. Hua's husband is an architect. Each had established careers in China. They left everything to come to America.

Conversion: In China, Hua had not been religious. She had been in America about one year before becoming a Christian. When asked what attracted her to Christianity, Hua explained that it was the kind, friendly caring atmosphere of the church. She had heard of a church that offered English lessons and thought it would help her learn American culture. When she began to attend, she found people who were kind and friendly and who wanted to help her. They wanted nothing in return. When asked why she had not been interested in Christianity while in China, Hua said that while she had been curious and had attended a Christian worship service while still in China, the message had not stood out as something that would really help her. But in America, with nothing, with practically no language skills and not understanding the culture, the message of a God who cared and who was there to help, and a Christian family that was also there to help, was something that would make a difference in her life. Christian love and kindness made a difference during a difficult time and Hua became a Christian.

Advice: When asked what advice she would give to church leaders who were interested in reaching out to immigrants, Hua said that church leaders must get to know people individually, to develop a friendship, to help, to share in their lives. She also said it was important not to push or expect decisions or responses too quickly, to allow people to observe, to understand.

3. Background: Peter Wang is a 66 year old male from China. He came to America in 2003, when he was 64. He came here to join his son who had immigrated earlier and who was a Christian. Peter has a Bechelor's degree but is now retired. In China, Peter had not become a Christian, though his mother had been a Christian. After being here about one year, Peter was converted.

Conversion: When asked what drew him to Christianity, Peter said he recognized the presence of spiritual needs in his life that were not being met. His mother's influence on him early in his life, and more recently his son's influence on him, led him to investigate Christianity. When asked what had been the most effective thing the church had done to draw him to Christianity, Peter spoke of the kindness of Christians who taught him English and the Bible. He appreciated that they had not pushed him for a quick response, but had given him time to observe, learn and understand.

Advice: When asked what advice he had for church leaders who want to work with immigrants, Peter did not feel he had enough insight to offer an opinion.

4. Background: Souli is a 41 year old female from Laos. She arrived here with her family in 1979 when she was 14 years old. They had fled Laos after the communist take over and had gone to Thailand and then to the Philippines (living in refugee camps) before arriving in Chicago. They had been extremely poor in Laos and their time in Thailand and the Philippines had not been much better. Officially her family was Buddhist, but on a practical level there was no religion to speak of. Their lives were consumed in the process of daily survival.

When Souli arrived in America she did not speak English and understood nothing of our culture. Though she had had no formal schooling in Laos, since she was 14 she was put into the eighth grade. By the time Souli had graduated from high school she could speak, read and write English. She has completed some college but has not earned a degree. Though Souli has not yet become an American Citizen, she plans to.

Conversion: It was 20 years before Souli was converted to Christianity. Souli's life in America before becoming a Christian continued to be scarred by suffering and hardship. Her mother died of cancer; she experienced a bad marriage. She was hurting and confused. Her conversion grew out of the kindness that was extended to her by Christians who were friendly, kind, patient and helpful. They cared about her as a person. They taught her the Bible and were her friends. When asked about the most important thing the church did for her on her journey toward Christian faith, Souli said Christians encouraged her, loved her, and comforted her.

Advice: When asked what advice she would give church leaders about reaching out to immigrants, Souli said, "to help them." She said the man who helped her a lot was as much a "social worker" as he was a minister. She added that people's physical needs must be met before they are ready to hear about their spiritual needs.

5. Background: Boun is a 49 year old male from Laos. He came to America 1980 when he was 23 years old. He left his country because after the communist takeover there was no freedom. He came to America to start a new life in a free country. In Laos, Boun had completed a high school education. He first entered the U.S. in California and eventually moved to Texas where he had an uncle who was a Christian. After five years in America, Boun was converted from Buddhism to Christianity.

Conversion: Boun's conversion to Christianity came through the efforts of his uncle who taught him after bringing him to Texas. The church helped Boun find a job and get settled. As his uncle began to teach him, Boun began to see the differences between Buddhism and Christianity. He became convinced that God, though Jesus, could do for him that which Buddha could not—save him from sin and secure his afterlife. When asked what the church had done to help him along in his journey toward Christian faith, Boun said they helped him get a job and get settled in. That made an important impression on him.

Advice: When asked what advice he would give to church leaders about outreach to immigrants, Boun said, "help them." Provide food, clothing. Help with housing. Then teach the Bible, teach Jesus.

6. Background: Lee is a 41 year old male from Laos. He came to this country with his family in 1987 when he was 22 years old. Lee's family left Laos to escape political oppression. Lee was in his third year of university studies when he left Laos and came to Texas. Lee was a Muslim. His father, who was half Indian, was a Muslim who required his family to keep Islamic ritual. Lee's father died, however, when Lee was nine and there was no mosque near Lee's home so Lee's Islamic training was minimal.

Conversion: Lee was converted to Christianity after only one year in this country. He said it was the kindness and love of Christians that drew him to faith. People who did not know him and wanted nothing from him cared about him. Thinking back, Lee now understands that he was seeing Christian love in action, faith and love being lived out in a meaningful way. That is what led him to Christ. Lee also said that the church taught him with teaching and preaching that were relevant to his life at the time.

Advice: When asked what advice he would give church leaders wanting to reach immigrants with the gospel, Lee said, that Christianity must be demonstrated, that leaders must help people through difficult times.

7. Background: Nelson is a 40 year old man from Laos. Nelson came to the U.S. (Texas) with his parents in 1983 when he was 17 years old. His parents left Laos in the midst of social and political turmoil looking for a better life in America. Nelson had a high school education and was a Buddhist.

Conversion: Nelson lived in Texas for two years before he became a Christian. At first, it appeared to him that everyone was a Christian and that the easiest thing for him to do, and the best way for him to fit in, was to become a Christian. Nelson, like many young people who want to belong, became a Christian at nineteen without the real relationship with God that ought to accompany a Christian commitment. Over the next five years Nelson came to understand what it really meant to be a believer. When asked what the most crucial thing was that the church had done for him in his faith journey, Nelson said it had been teaching him the Bible.

Advice: When asked what advice he would give to church leaders who wanted to reach out effectively to immigrants, Nelson said that the church should demonstrate Christian faith and love by patiently helping immigrants in whatever ways they can.

8. Background: Davone is a 37 year old female from Laos. Davone came to the U.S. in 1979 when she was only ten years old. Her father had been a soldier in Laos before deciding to leave his war-torn country with his family. They entered the U.S. in Chicago, Illinois. Being only ten years old and from a country where it was a struggle just to stay alive, Davone had no formal education. Officially her family was Buddhist, but like so many others from that time and place, their official religion was a mere formality with no practical meaning. Having arrived when she was only ten years old, Davone learned English quickly, finishing high school and going on to earn a Bachelor's degree from an American university.

Conversion: Davone became a Christian in 1996 as she struggled to understand and make sense of life. Her mother had died of cancer and she was looking for answers. She had taken a college course in Eastern Religions and realized that they offered few answers to the kinds of questions she was asking. Then she studied Christianity. It turned out to be what she had been looking for.

When asked what the church did that was effective in helping her on her faith journey, Davone felt Bible study had been what she had needed. The immigration-related struggles she had experienced as a child (language, culture, etc.) were past. What she needed now was truth to live by. But she remembered how kind the Christians had been to them when they had first arrived in Chicago. They had taught them how to shop, how to use appliances. They had taken them to church. They had been kind and helpful. The seeds of kindness planted years before were bearing fruit.

Advice: When asked what advice she would give to church leaders who wanted to work effectively among immigrants Davone remembered what the church had done for her family. That's how the church should reach out to immigrants—help them. Be kind to them.

9. Background: Vie is a 40 year old female from Laos. She came to the U.S. in 1979 with her family when she was 13. Her family left Laos because of political unrest. After spending nearly three years in various relocation camps, Vie and her family arrived in Chicago. Like most Laotians, she was officially Buddhist. For all practical purposes, however, she had no religion. She had received little schooling.

Conversion: Vie was converted to Christianity about ten years after immigrating to the U.S. She became a U.S. citizen in 1999. When asked what prompted her to become a Christian, Vie said that her initial motivation was to belong to something, to better herself and her family. When asked how the church had influenced her decision to become a Christian, Vie said that (even though she had been in the U.S. nearly ten years) the church helped financially with relocation expenses (from Minnesota to Texas) and assisted her in finding a job. After she had relocated, the church provided her with a tutor each Saturday to teach her the Bible.

Advice: When asked what advice she would give to church leaders who wanted to work effectively with immigrants, Vie said that English classes were important, and that teenagers should be given special attention. The teen years are difficult enough as it is. Immigration as a teen makes it an even more difficult time. Special classes and activities for teen immigrants would be very helpful. Get them involved; get them talking.

10. Background: Kets is a 43 year old female from Laos. Kets was 16 when she came to the U.S. in 1979. She entered the country in Chicago after spending two years in relocation camps. Her family had to flee Laos because of political oppression. She was a Buddhist. She had an elementary education.

Conversion: Kets was converted to Christianity after moving to Texas. She had been in the U.S. for nine years. When asked what factors had led to her conversion Kets said that the Christians were good people who helped others. They helped her find a job. They taught her the Word of God, which helped her and her family. When asked what the church had done that had influenced her the most in her decision to embrace Christianity, Kets said that the physical help she received and the opportunity to be involved with Christians at church had influenced her. The Christians did not just teach her; they spent time with her. They were friends.

Advice: When asked what advice she would give to church leaders who want to work effectively with immigrants, Kets said that church leaders need to demonstrate the love and faith of Christianity by helping with physical needs. The commitment to help others must be present first. Then teach them about God. Show first, then teach.

11. Background: Peter is a 41 year old male from Cambodia. Peter came to the U.S. in 1981 when he was 16. The war and the "killing fields" simply made it too dangerous to stay in Cambodia. At the time of his immigration to the U.S., Peter had a sixth grade education. Peter is now a school teacher working on his master's degree. Texas was his point of entry into the U.S. In 1986 Peter became an American citizen.

Conversion: Peter was a Buddhist in Cambodia, though as was often the case in that part of the world at that time, he was a Buddhist in name only. He was converted to conservative Christianity about three years after his arrival in the States. When asked what drew him to Christianity, Peter said that it was seeing people living their faith, seeing Christianity being exemplified.

Advice: When asked what advice he would give to church leaders who wanted to reach out effectively to immigrants, Peter said there were four things to do:

1. learn the culture of the people they want to reach,
2. understand why they immigrated to America,
3. find out what kind of help they need,
4. attempt to teach them only after you understand them and have helped them.

12. Background: Chun is a 53 year old male from Cambodia. Chun came to the U.S. in 1976 when he was 23. In Cambodia, Chun's family, his parents and siblings, were killed. He escaped his country in order to survive. After spending time in a refugee camp in Thailand, he was allowed to enter the U.S. Texas was his point of entry. Chun had a middle school education and was a Buddhist. In 1990 Chun became an American citizen.

Conversion: Chun became a Christian in 1986, but Chun explained that his conversion journey had begun in the Thai refugee camps, where Christian missionaries helped the people. There were no Buddhists there to help them; nor were there Muslims. Only Christians. Later, when Chun arrived in the U.S., Christians were there again to help him, to help him learn English, learn the culture, to find a job, to provide transportation to the doctor when someone was ill. Over the years, Christians helped him a lot. So Chun, over the angry objections of the rest of his Buddhist family members, became a Christian.

Advice: When asked what advice he would give church leaders who wanted to reach out to immigrants, Chun said, "help them and then wait." Give them time to think, to learn, to respond. Some, he said, will not be interested. Help them anyway. Don't push them.

13. Background: Van is a 48 year old male from Cambodia. He came here in 1979 when he was 22 years old. Like so many others, he came to escape the killing and suffering. Van's point of entry into the U.S. was Texas. He had some college when he arrived. In 1986 he became an American citizen.

Conversion: In Cambodia, Van was a Buddhist—officially. On a day-to-day basis, he had no religion. Van actually became a Christian while in the refugee camp in Thailand. As a university student, he was looking for answers. The war and the suffering of so many people prompted serious questions and deep longings within him. There was so much suffering. Then a missionary came to the camp. She came to help. Van saw her live the message, then he heard her preach the message. He learned of God and Jesus and found that Christianity answered many of his questions. He became a believer.

Advice: When asked what advice he had for church leaders, Van said that Christians should express unconditional love for new immigrants, letting them see the way of Christ. Then, after they see, they will be ready to hear. He advised that Christians be open to other cultural ways of thinking and living, that Christians not criticize immigrants because they are different. They must be given time to understand. The message of sin and death and salvation through the death of Jesus is very strange to people who come from non-Christian cultures. It takes a long time to understand and accept.

14. Background: Sokha is a 45 year old female from Cambodia who came to the U.S. in 1981 when she was 21. She left her country to escape the communists and to be free. She had been a Buddhist. In 1991 she became an American citizen. Her U.S point of entry was Texas, but only after a time in a Thai refugee camp.
Conversion: Sokha became a Christian while she was still in the refugee camp. The Christian missionaries there helped and taught her.
Advice: When asked advice she had for church leaders regarding working with immigrants, Sokha said Christians should learn the culture of the immigrants. Then, help them with their needs—food, shelter, etc. Show them Jesus' love. Use the Bible to teach them English.

15. Background: Vanthy is a 42 year old female from Cambodia who came to the U.S. in 1981 when she was 17. Her parents were killed in the war. She had a high school education and was a Buddhist. Her point of entry was Texas. In 1986, Vanthy became an American citizen.
Conversion: Vanty's immigration was sponsored by a Christian couple with whom she lived for a time after her arrival. They loved her like a daughter and their love for her turned her heart to Jesus.
Advice: When asked what advice she had for church leaders who want to work with immigrants, Vanthy said to love

them, to become friends with them so they know someone cares. Help them and love them.

16. Background: Kim is a 66 year old female from Cambodia. She came to the U.S. in 1981 when she was 40 years old. She left her home country because she wanted freedom for her children, and an education. Kim had a Bachelor's degree and was a nurse. She was a Buddhist. In 1986 she became a U.S. citizen.

Conversion: Kim's immigration to America was by way of the Philippines, where she stayed in a refugee camp for a time. She was converted while in the refugee camp. When asked why she converted, Kim said that Buddhism was good, but Christianity was better because Christians helped others. The refugees were given food and everything they needed by Christian missionaries. This love drew her to Christianity.

Advice: When asked what advice she would give church leaders who wanted to work with immigrants, Kim said that Christians must show immigrants unconditional love. Help them with what they need. When they are sick, visit them. Show them God's love.

17. Background: Socheat is a 44 year old female from Cambodia who came to the U.S. in 1981 when she was 19. Her father had been in politics and when the communists took over her family had to flee. Socheat had a high school education and was a Buddhist. Her point of entry into the country was Texas. In 1986 she became an American citizen.

Conversion: Like other refugees, Socheat heard about Jesus while in the refugee camps. She married a man who had become a Christian and he taught and converted her.

Advice: When asked what advice she would give regarding effective outreach among immigrants, Socheat said that Christians must find ways to show immigrants that God has sent them to tell the story of Jesus. Then God will open their hearts.

18. Background: Catalina is a 33 year old female from Mexico. She came to the U.S. in 1989 at the age of 17. She is a legal resident. She immigrated to the U.S., Texas being her point of entry, in hopes of a better life for herself. She came with a basic elementary school education and other than English lessons has not yet been able to continue her education.

Conversion: Catalina was Catholic when she came to the U.S. It was 15 years before she was converted to conservative protestant Christianity, though she had been investigating and learning for four years before making a commitment. When asked what initially interested her in a very different expression of Christian faith, Catalina said that it was seeing Christians who were out in the community doing something, making a difference. The Christians [of the church she later became a member of] rented an apartment in her complex and came during the week to teach classes on parenting skills, health, and other general things. They provided child care so the mothers could go shopping and so forth. Then on Sundays, they returned and taught a Bible lesson. Catalina was impressed by their kindness.

Advice: When asked what advice she would give to church leaders who want to reach out to immigrants, Catalina said to focus on the children, providing programs of education and recreation (and day care) with a biblical and Christian focus.

19. Background: Oscar is a 47 year old male from Colombia. Oscar came to the U.S., to Florida, in 1980 as a college student to study international marketing. He was Catholic. He was converted to conservative protestant Christianity after one year. Oscar went back to Colombia for a few years before returning again to the U.S. in 1992. Since returning, Oscar has earned an MBA and will become a U.S. citizen in 2006.

Conversion: When asked what led him to be interested in a form of Christianity different from Catholicism, Oscar explained that he had been invited to a Christian concert and liked the music. He liked the people there, too, and decided he would go to the church that had put on the concert to see what it was like. When he went, he found the preaching to be very practical, down-to-earth and useful. He liked it. In about a year be was converted.

Advice: When asked what advice he had for church leaders who want to work with immigrants, Oscar said not to start out by talking about religion. Begin by being friends. Give them time to get to know you, to trust you.

20. Background: Angel is a 42 year old male from Mexico. Angel came to the U.S. in 1983 when he was 19. He came with a high school education to visit his brother and to attend college to study English. His entry point was Texas. He was Catholic. Angel is not yet a citizen but plans to become a citizen.

Conversion: After 2 years Angel was converted to conservative protestant Christianity. When asked what led to his conversion, he said that he had not been interested in religion, but his brother had been studying with some Christians who came to the house to study. His older brother was converted and baptized and that made Angel start thinking. He then began studying the Bible himself. He came to see the importance of spiritual things and was converted.

Advice: When asked what advice he had for church leaders who want to work with immigrants Angel said:

1. be friends with them,
2. respect their current beliefs,

3. help them—rent, food, transportation, finding a job—whatever. Be a genuine friend, not just someone trying to win a convert.

21. Background: Jose Luis is a 50 year old male from Mexico. He came to the U.S. in 1974 when he was 18. He entered the U.S. in Texas intending to go to college. But he had no money and had to find work. College never happened. Jose Luis is not yet a citizen but has begun the process and will become a citizen in 2006.

Conversion: In Mexico, Jose Luis' family was not religious. They believed in God but did not attend church. They did not claim to be Catholics. Jose Luis was in the U.S. for 7 years before he became a Christian. When asked what led to his conversion, Jose Luis explained that he had felt empty and was searching for something to give his life meaning. Nothing seemed to work. His wife began studying the Bible with people from her friend's church and Jose Luis eventually got interested. As he began studying the Bible, things began to make sense to him. Christianity was what he had been looking for. Jose Luis was converted.

Advice: When asked what advice he had for church leaders who wanted to work effectively with immigrants, Jose Luis said to learn and use their language. Understand their culture so you can approach them in ways that makes sense to them.

22. Background: Genoveva is a 49 year old female from Mexico. She came to the U.S. in 1974 when she was 17. Genoveva's father was already here and she came with the rest of her family to join her father. Genoveva had a high school education. Her family was officially Catholic, but were not really practicing Catholics.

Conversion: Genoveva was converted after seven years in the U.S. A neighbor boy who was a friend of her son, invited him to come to church with him. Genoveva wanted to go with him so she asked the little boy's mother if she could go as well. Her neighbor was enthusiastic about her coming along with her son. She enjoyed the worship assembly and the people, and when someone from the church offered to study the Bible with her she agreed. Eventually she was converted.

Advice: When asked what advice she would give church leaders who wanted to work effectively with immigrants, Genoveva said to get to know them. Give them time to trust you. Invite them to church but do not attack their current religion. She explained that in her culture religion is a family tradition. When you criticize someone's religion you are criticizing their family, which throws up barriers. Do not criticize. Give them time to learn, understand and decide for themselves.

23. Background: Juan Paulo is a 26 year old male from Colombia. Juan came to the U.S. in 1999 when he was 19 to join the rest of his family who was already here. Juan entered the U.S. in Texas and had completed 1 year of college when he arrived. He has been able to take a few additional college courses while working. He plans to become a U.S. citizen. Juan Paulo was not religious in Colombia. His parents, however, were Gnostics.

Conversion: Juan Paulo was here for four years before becoming a Christian. When asked what led him to begin thinking about Christianity, Juan explained that he had always been interested in spiritual things. He read a lot and talked with his Christian friends about Christianity. One day he asked his friends if they would study the Bible with him so he could know more about God.

Advice: When asked what advice he would give to church leaders who want to work effectively with immigrants, Juan said that they must utilize small groups for home Bible studies. He also felt that in the Latino community radio spots would be helpful.

24. Background: Roger is a 28 year old male from Honduras. Roger came to the U.S. in 1998 when he was 20. He had been invited to the U.S. by his uncle who already lived here. Roger entered the U.S. in Texas. He had not finished high school in Honduras and has not been able to complete high school yet, though he has taken some English classes and work-related technical courses.

Conversion: Roger was a Catholic in Honduras, though not very active. He was converted only two months after leaving Honduras. His journey to the U.S. took a long time and while in Mexico (on his way to Texas) he met some Christians who got him to thinking about getting closer to God. They began studying the Bible with him, helping him understand spiritual things. When he arrived in the U.S. he was ready to be baptized.

Advice: When asked what advice he had for church leaders who want to work with immigrants, Roger said that immigrants need help with basic needs—language, culture job, transportation and so forth. Some have family or sponsors who can help. Some do not. They need friends who will help them. Programs for culture and language learning are also helpful.

25. Background: Elvia is a 45 year old female from Mexico. Elvia came to the U.S. in 1981 when she was 20. She entered the U.S. in Texas with her new husband who had gone to Mexico to marry her. He was a legal resident who lived in Texas, so Elvia entered the country with him. She had completed two years of university at the time—studying business. Since then she has taken several special HR courses. In 2000 Elvia became a U.S. citizen.

Conversion: Elvia was a Catholic in Mexico, but not very active. She was converted to a conservative protestant expression of the Christian faith after being in the U.S. for nine years. Elvia had answered her door one day to find a lady selling encyclopedias. Elvia said she didn't speak

English. The woman said that was no problem because she spoke Spanish. Elvia let her in and listened for a while before telling the woman she did not want to buy encyclopedias. The woman accepted her comment and then asked her if she could come by and pick her up and take her to church. Elvia, who was pregnant at the time said she was not supposed to leave the house. Elvia's eight year old daughter was home so the woman asked if she could give her daughter a ride to church. Elvia said she could. The daughter liked it and continued attending with the lady. After Elvia's baby was born she went with her daughter to the woman's church. Elvia enjoyed it as well. She began studying and was converted.

Advice: When asked what advice she would give church leaders about working with immigrants, Elvia said they should make use of small groups for Bible studies and be sure to invite people to church and to home Bible studies.

26. Background: Ermilo is a 53 male from Mexico. Ermilo came to the U.S. in 1968 when he was 15 to escape the poverty of Mexico and build a better life for himself. He had completed primary school. Ermilo entered the U.S. in Texas and has completed a number of specialized work-related technical courses. Ermilo was raised a Catholic but was not active in the Catholic faith.

Conversion: Ermilo was converted to a conservative protestant expression of the Christian faith after being in the U.S. for 37 years. When asked what led him to his conversion experience, Ermilo said that his life was empty. He felt empty, lonely, disconnected. So he began looking for something. His wife, who had been experiencing the same feelings, had begun studying the Bible with some Christian friends and Ermilo began sitting in on the study. That Bible study led to his conversion.

Advice: When asked what advice he would give to church leaders who want to work with immigrants, Ermilo said they should take advantage of Spanish radio, putting on religious programming that explained biblical Christianity and use a call-in format to give general counseling advice.

27. Background: Maricela is a 39 year old female from Mexico. She came to the U.S. in 1987 when she was 20. She had completed two years of college. Maricela entered the U.S. in California to continue her education. That got sidetracked, however, with the need to earn a living. She has attended a number of job-related technical training courses.

Conversion: Maricela grew up a Catholic and was very active in the Catholic church in Mexico. After coming to the U.S., however, she was not as active and eventually lost interest. Maricela was converted to a conservative protestant expression of the Christian faith 19 years after she immigrated to the U.S. Maricela was feeling a void in her life. Her spiritual needs were not being met. A friend told her about a group of Christians she had found who were not judgmental, but who would accept her for who she was and study the Bible with her. Maricela went to church with her friend and found that the Christians there were friendly and open. Maricela found what she was looking for.

Advice: When asked what advice she has for church leaders who want to work with immigrants, Maricela said they should be friendly, sincere and non-judgmental as they work with immigrants.

28. Background: Barbara is a 48 year old female from Mexico. She came to the U.S. in 1973 with an older sister when she was 14 looking for a better life. Barbara had finished primary school in Mexico. After immigrating to Texas she was able to finish high school. Barbara is in the process of becoming a citizen. Officially, Barbara was a Catholic while in Mexico, but did not practice her traditional religion in any real way. Barbara had been in the U.S. about nine years before being converted to a conservative Protestant expression of the Christian faith.

Conversion: Barbara had been a young girl when she came to the U.S. and did not have adequate supervision. By the time she was a young woman, she had come to feel alone, like no one cared. She met a family of Christians that cared about her and their love and care changed her life. She became a Christian.

Advice: When asked what advice she had for church leaders who want to work with immigrants, Barbara said that they needed to be friends first. There should be no other motives—just be friends. Everything else comes later.

29. Background: Juan is a 30 year old male from Mexico. He came to the U.S. in 1994 when he was 18. Juan's father already lived in the U.S. and when Juan graduated from high school his father brought him to the U.S. to find a job. Juan entered the U.S. in Texas. Juan was raised a Catholic but was not active in that faith. He was converted to a conservative protestant expression of Christianity two years after coming to the States.

Conversions: When asked what led him to rethink his faith, Juan said that he had felt empty, depressed, lonely. He met a girl (who later became his wife) who invited him to church. He began to see the difference between life with God and life without God. He chose a life of faith.

Advice: When asked what advice he had for churches that want to work with immigrants, Juan said it was essential for church leaders to get to know the people they wanted to reach—to know them culturally and socially.

30. Background: Alex is a 36 year old male from Honduras. He came to the U.S. in 1986 when he was 16. He came with his mother to the U.S. in search of a better life. At that time, Alex did not like the idea of immigrating. Alex and his mother entered the U.S. in Texas. He had completed high school. Alex became a citizen in 2004 and is currently working on his CFP (Certified Financial Planner) certification at Texas A & M.

Conversion: Alex had been raised a Catholic and had been active in the church when he was young. But as he became a teenager he lost interest. Alex had been in the U.S. about nine years before being converted. When asked what led to his conversion, Alex explained that he had a child and knew he needed to make some changes. He knew he needed guidance to be the father he wanted to be. Alex's cousin, who had been "wild" when younger, had changed completely when he became a Christian. He invited Alex to church. Alex went and attended a small group Bible class that that utilized a discussion format. Alex liked being able to ask questions and express his opinion. Alex had been looking for something but didn't know what. When he found Christianity he knew that was what he needed and wanted.

Advice: When asked what advice he had for church leaders who want to work with immigrants, Alex said they must use small groups. They need to love people and care for them, then those people will come to a small group home study. Alex also said to use the immigrant network to reach into a community and build relationships.

31. Background: Sinforiano is a 48 year old male who came to the U.S. from Honduras in 1982 when he was 24. He left his family behind and came looking for work with the idea he would stay two years, make some money and return home. But he did not return home. When he could, he brought his family here to join him. Sinforiano entered the U.S. in Texas with a primary-level education. He studied English and over the years took a series of job-related technical courses. In 2000, Sinforiano became a U.S. citizen.

Conversion: Sinforiano had been a Catholic in Honduras. He had been very active in the church but his faith (theology) had never really been clear. So it was not very helpful when life became difficult. That lack of clarity followed him to the U.S. and plagued him for the next 19 years. On a visit back to Honduras, where his two grown daughters lived, he went with them to an evangelical church. He liked what he heard. It made sense. Could this be the clarity that had eluded him for so long? He came back to the States and continued his search, visiting protestant churches, listening for a clear message. He found a church where the message was clear and helpful and was converted to a conservative protestant expression of the Christian faith.

Advice: When asked what advice he had for church leaders wanting to work with immigrants, Sinforiano said that church leaders must understand what it is like to be the people (the immigrants) with whom they wish to work. The church must get to know the people they want to reach out to because you can't reach people you don't understand.

32. Background: Yolanda is a 42 year old female from Mexico. She came to the U.S. in 1988 when she was 25 looking for a better life for herself and her daughter. California was their point of entry into the U.S. Yolanda had a ninth grade education at that time.

Conversion: Yolanda had been raised a Catholic but was not active in that faith. She had been in the U.S. six years before being converted. When asked what led to her conversion she explained that her husband had become a Christian and she saw the difference in his life. She wanted the benefits of Christianity in her life as well.

Advice: When asked what advice she would have for church leaders who want to work with immigrants, Yolanda said that it was important to use small groups.

33. Background: Samuel is a 38 year old male from Mexico who immigrated to the U.S. in 1983 when he was 15 years old. He had an eighth grade education and came looking for an opportunity to build a better life. Texas was his point of entry into the U.S. In 1998 Samuel became a U.S. citizen.

Conversion: Samuel had been raised a Catholic and had been in the U.S. 23 years before being converted. When asked what led to his conversion, Samuel explained that he had been experiencing difficulties in his life. He felt alone, was making bad decisions and was depressed. He felt he needed guidance, needed God in his life. Samuel's girlfriend had been experiencing some of the same kinds of problems. A friend of hers had invited her to church and she had found it helpful. She invited Samuel. He went and found it helpful as well. After attending for a while and studying the Bible, Samuel was converted.

Advice: When asked what advice he would have for church leaders wanting to work with immigrants, Samuel said that they needed to make friends with people, then invite them to small group home studies.

34. Background: Raul is a 44 year old male from Mexico who immigrated to the U.S. in 1986 when he was 24 years old. He was looking for better economic and educational opportunities for his family. Raul had an eighth grade education. Raul has taken English classes since coming to the U.S. but has had no opportunity to further his education formally. In 1997 he became a citizen.

Conversion: Raul grew up with no religion and was in the U.S. for six years before being converted. When asked what led to his conversion, Raul explained that he had been staying with some friends. One Sunday morning he answered a knock on the door. It was a minister looking for the friends with whom he was staying. The minister had stopped by to bring them to church. But they had left and were not there. The minister invited Raul to join him at church. Raul did not feel well—he had been out drinking the night before—but said he would go next Sunday. Next week the minister came to give him a ride and he went. It got him to thinking about spiritual things and his life and eventually he decided to give his life to the Lord.

Advice: When asked what advice he would have for church leaders who want to work with immigrants, Raul explained that Latinos were open to door to door evangelism. Many people would come to church or a small study group if invited by someone who came to their door.

35. Background: Esther is a 47 year old female from Colombia. She came to the U.S. in 1999 when she was 40. A Colombian man who had been a U.S. resident for many years returned to Colombia for a vacation. The two met while he was there and Esther married him and returned to the States (Texas) with her new husband. She had a high school education and was Catholic. Esther is not yet an American citizen but plans to become one.

Conversion: Esther had been in the U.S. for five years before she was converted to a conservative protestant expression of the Christian faith. When asked what led to her conversion, Esther explained that she had been sick. Some Christians she had met, also from Colombia, began praying for her and invited her to church. When Esther felt well enough to go, she found a very friendly group of people who were interested in her and cared about her. Their love and concern impressed her. She began to study the Bible and decided to change her life by becoming a committed Christian.

Advice: When asked what advice she would give church leaders who want to work with immigrants, Esther said to be friends with the people and let them see God working in your life.

36. Background: Olga is a sixty year old female from Mexico. She came to the U.S. in 1970 when she was 24. She came to work. She entered the U.S. in Texas with a seventh grade education. She has become a U.S. citizen. Olga grew up as a Catholic.

Conversion: Olga was converted to conservative protestant Christianity after seven years in the U.S. When asked what led to her conversion, Olga explained that she had been thinking about spiritual matters but had not done anything about it. One day she was working in the yard and some people knocking on doors in the community stopped to talk with her. She agreed to study the Bible with them and in time came to see that she wanted to change her life.

Advice: When asked what advice she would give to church leaders who want to work with immigrants, Olga said the Christians must be friendly. They must be able to teach people from the Bible.

37. Background: Orlando is a 54 year old male from Colombia. He came to the U.S. in 1984 when he was 33, looking for better living and working conditions. He had a high school education and was Catholic. He entered the U.S. in Texas. In 1999 Orlando became a U.S. citizen.

Conversion: Orlando had been in the U.S. for 20 years before being converted. When asked what led to his conversion, he said that he had gone through a divorce and was having some health issues. The doctor had told him he might need open heart surgery. Through some mutual friends who were Christians, Orlando met a minister and one other church leader. They took an interest in him. They began praying for his health (for him and with him) and invited him to a dinner at church. Orlando told them he would come to the dinner but he was not interested in changing his religion. They told him that was fine. They just wanted him to come and enjoy the dinner. Orlando met a lot of people who were friendly and who accepted him. He liked them. He began attending church and finally began studying the Bible. Eventually he was converted.

Advice: When asked what advice he would give church leaders about working with immigrants, Orlando said, "first be friends." Take time to get to know someone and to build a relationship. Then you can teach them later.

38. Background: Julia is an 82 year old female from Mexico. She came to the U.S. in 1970 when she was 46. She had met and married a man from Texas so she (and her two daughters) came with him to live in Texas. She had a primary school education and was Catholic. In 1993 Julia became a citizen.

Conversion: Julia had been in the U.S. six years before being converted. When asked what led to her conversion she explained that her daughters had been converted after they started attending a church in Dallas. Her daughters wanted to study the Bible with her. She agreed and studying the Bible led her to be converted as her daughters had been.

Advice: When asked what advice she had for church leaders who want to work effectively with immigrants, Julia said that Christians must let other people get to know them. People who are not yet Christians need to see Christianity at work in your life. Only after they "see" are they ready to study the Bible.

39. Background: Esthela is a 49 year old female from Mexico. She came to the U.S. in 1974 when she was 16. She came as a student. She was in the eleventh grade and entered the U.S. in Chicago, IL. She now has a college degree and is a citizen.

Conversion: Esthela was raised a Catholic but was converted to a conservative protestant expression of the Christian faith after having been in the U.S. for 17 years. When asked what led to her conversion, Esthela explained that although she was married and had children, her life lacked purpose. She felt she needed something else. She began searching by attending different churches. Some she attended made her feel uncomfortable in their approach to spiritual matters. A friend invited her to church and she went with her friend. This group of Christians made her feel welcome and comfortable. Eventually she studied the Bible with them and was converted.

Advice: When asked what advice she had for church leaders who want to work with immigrants, Esthela said that people must see that Christians love them and love each other. Christians must not criticize too much and must support the people. Loving them is the key.

40. Background: David is a 59 year old male from Mexico. David came to the U.S. in 1981 looking for work. He had been working as an electrician in Saudi Arabia. When his job there ended he came here, entering the U.S. in Texas. He had a diploma that qualified him as an electrician. David became a citizen in 1989.

Conversion: David was raised a Catholic. After 20 years in the U.S. he was converted to a conservative form of protestant Christianity. When asked what led to that conversion, David explained that a group of people who were all Catholics had begun studying the Bible and found a number of things there that were different from the practices of the Catholic church. They wanted to do what they found in the Bible. When they went to the priest to talk about those things, he was angry and told them to leave the church. Then, later, when David encountered some marriage difficulties, he went to a Catholic priest for help and was told to let his wife go and not worry about it. In frustration, David began visiting other churches and found a group of believers who studied the Bible and tried to live and worship according to it. Eventually he was converted.

Advice: When asked what advice he had for church leaders who want to work with immigrants, David said he believed radio was an effective medium for outreach. Keep the message simple. Don't ask for money. Be careful not to tell them to change their religion. Instead, invite them to worship and activities and let them see the differences for themselves.

41. Background: Gloria is a 57 year old female from Honduras. She came to the U.S. in 1970 when she was 21 years old. Initially she came to visit a cousin. But she met a man here and after returning to Honduras she eventually returned to the U.S. to get married. She entered the U.S. in California. Educationally, Gloria had been trained to be a secretary. In 1990 she became a U.S. citizen.
Conversion: Gloria had been raised a Catholic. In 1994, 24 years after coming here, Gloria was converted. When asked what led to her conversion, Gloria explained that her brother had been talking to her about spiritual things. Her sister bought her a Bible and she began reading it. Eventually, she understood that she needed to give her life to the Lord. Since being baptized she feels like a new person. She has peace.
Advice: When asked what advice she would give church leaders who want to work with immigrants, Gloria said church leaders need to go to people's homes to study with them and help them with their problems. They should not speak negatively about the Catholic church or any other church. They should also help immigrants understand the [civil] laws and help them feel more comfortable in their new country.

42. Background: Feisal is a 31 year old male from Honduras. He was 21 when he came to the U.S. in 1996. He entered the U.S. in Texas, looking for better economic opportunities. When he left Honduras, Feisal had completed four years of university and almost had his degree in engineering. He has not been able to finish his college degree yet but plans to. He has not yet become a citizen.

Conversion: Feisal was raised without any religion. But in the ten years he has been here he has come to see the need for the presence of God in his life. Feisal plans to be baptized soon. When asked what led him to this point of being ready to make a commitment to God, Feisal explained that his family had led him to the Lord. His wife is a Christian, as is his cousin. But he also experienced a difference in his life as he came to know God. Even though he still encounters difficulties in life, knowing God makes a difference.

Advice: When asked what advice Feisal had for church leaders who want to work with immigrants, Feisal said immigrants need to hear the truth about God. They need to hear a sincere proclamation from someone who truly cares about them, not from someone who is trying to increase church attendance or membership. Immigrants need to hear personal testimony about what God has done in the life of the person talking with them.

43. Background: Sonia is a 40 year old female from Mexico. Sonia came to the U.S. in 1988 when she was 22 years old. She had completed the first year of university and was working as an accountant. She entered the U.S. in Texas, looking for a better economic situation. She has not yet become an American citizen.

Conversion: Sonia was raised a Catholic but after 17 years in the U.S. was converted to a conservative protestant expression of the Christina faith. When asked what led up to her conversion, she explained that earlier in life she had not been interested in spiritual matters. But as she got older she felt an emptiness and knew she needed something to fill her soul. She began looking for God in different churches but could not find him. She wanted a church that was like the church she read about in the Bible. When she found one, she was converted.

Advice: When asked what advice she had for church leaders who want to work with immigrants, Sonia said there needs to be a lot of prayer. They need to follow the lead of the Holy Spirit as he directs outreach to people who do not yet know God.

44. Background: Luke is a 40 year old male from China. He came to the States in 1995, when he was 30, to work on his Ph.D. in microbiology. He entered the States in Texas with an M.A. He has completed his Ph.D. but has not become a U.S. citizen.

Conversion: In China, Luke had no religion. He was converted to Christianity after three years here in the U.S. When asked what led to his conversion, Luke explained that although he had no formal religion, he always knew there was something beyond this physical world, some creative power and presence, though he did not know what (or who) it was. He began reading the Bible because he was interested in all kinds of philosophy. So initially he was trying to understand a Christian philosophical perspective on life. But as he read, he became more and more interested, although he did not understand how everything fit together. Through a Christian fellowship community he joined, he met some church leaders who studied with him and helped him understand. But it was more than just intellectual understanding. It was relational. The fellowship they offered was important.

Advice: When asked what advice he had for church leaders who want to work effectively with immigrants, Luke said to develop a relationship and create plenty of opportunities for fellowship. Let them see Christianity at work and then let them ask questions.

45. Background: Bruce is a 39 year old male from Taiwan. He came to the U.S. in 1995 when he was 28. He came to work on his M.A. He entered the U.S. in Texas with a B.A. He is now working on his Ph.D. He has not become a citizen yet but may in the future.

Conversion: In Taiwan, Bruce had no formal religion, but believed in many gods and occasionally practiced various religious rituals. After being in the U.S. for about a year and a half he became a Christian. When asked why, Bruce explained that some friends he met after coming to U.S. were Christians. They invited him to spend the Christmas holidays with them. He was here to go to school and was alone. Their inviting him to their home for the holidays when the campus was closed and he had no where to go was very meaningful to him. His first exposure to Christianity was learning about Christmas. Eventually Bruce began going to the Student Christian Center on campus and enjoyed the fellowship. They helped him with language and cultural questions. When he encountered an emotional difficulty (breaking up with his girlfriend) his Christian friends were there to help with comfort and counseling. This led to his conversion.

An important part of the conversion process, Bruce said, was someone talking with him about spiritual concerns in Mandarin. English was good for the fellowship and friendship aspects, but when he needed to ask serious questions and listen to Bible answers, the conversation need to be in his heart language—Mandarin.

Advice: When asked what advice he had for church leaders who want to work effectively with immigrants, Bruce said:

1. be friends first and win their trust,
2. when, as friends, they begin to discuss life issues, this is a sign of trust and friendship and is a good time to begin talking with them about spiritual matters,
3. go slow and be patient; avoid being aggressive, pushing for a decision.

46. Background: J is a 46 year old female from China. She came to the U.S. in 1994 when she was 34 years old. She came first to Canada, then to Texas. Her initial reason for coming to the U.S. was to work on a graduate degree. She had a BA when she came.

J has a family and caring for them has taken all her energies. She has not yet completed her graduate studies. One day she will. In 2004 she became a U.S. citizen.

Conversion: In China, J had no formal religion. But after being in the U.S. one year she became a Christian. When asked what led to her conversion, J explained that her parents had instilled moral values in her and when she began reading the Bible she liked it. It made sense to her. She met some people who were Christians and they were kind to her. They invited her to church and when she went to worship she always felt at peace. That sense of inner peace and the kindness of Christians made her want to be a Christian.

Advice: When asked what advice she had for church leaders who want to work effectively with immigrants, J said:
1. first make friends—eat with them, let them trust you,
2. help them in any way you can,
3. then, after trust is established, you can teach them.

47. Background: Jim is a 42 year old male from Taiwan. He came to the U.S. in 1988 when he was 24. He entered the States in Texas having completed some college. His purpose in coming here was to go to school. Jim now has a Ph.D. in Electrical Engineering. He has not yet become a citizen.

Conversion: Jim had no religion in Taiwan and was not converted for 15 years. When asked what led to his conversion, Jim explained that his sister who had come to the States before him had become a Christian and told him of God's love for him. This was the first time he had heard such a thing. He began attending a Friday night Bible study but was not really interested in going to church. Jim enjoyed the fellowship of the small group study and would participate. He went to Bible studies for 12 years but would not give himself to the Lord because he did not feel God's presence in his life. At that point in his life there was no "personal experience" kind of proof of God's love or presence. Until he felt it he would make no commitment. He got married to a Christian woman. After finishing his Ph.D. he got a job, but after seven months got laid off. This was traumatic for him and one day he asked his wife how she knew God was there. She told him to pray. Jim had intentionally not prayed for nearly 15 years. He was waiting for God to make himself known first. He was so desperate that he went to the lab and prayed. God made his presence known (felt) to Jim and that was enough for Jim. He became a believer and made a commitment.

Advice: When asked what advice he had for church leaders who want to work effectively with immigrants, Jim said:
1. get to know them,
2. don't pressure them for a decision
3. accept them, include them, be patient.

48. Background: Naomi is a 32 year old female from Taiwan. She came to the States in 1997 when she was 23. She entered the U.S. in California to study. She had an MA and came to work on her Ph.D. She has not become a citizen.

Conversion: In Taiwan, Naomi was a Daoist. But after only two years in the U.S. she became a Christian. When asked what led to her conversion, Naomi explained that she encountered some relationship problems that made her realize that she was not in control of everything in her life. She was alone and empty and felt useless. She needed comfort. She needed God to fill the emptiness inside. Through the Taiwanese Student Campus Association Naomi met a lady who was a Christian. Naomi was making some changes in her life and needed a place to spend the night (a Saturday night) and the lady Naomi had just met invited

Naomi to stay with her. Sunday morning Naomi asked if she could go to church with the lady. Naomi eventually became a Christian in that church.

Advice: When asked what advice she had for church leaders who want to work effectively with immigrants, Naomi said, Christians need to know and respect the culture of the people with whom they wish to work. They must try to connect Christ to the people's culture. Immigrants must be thought of as equals and include them in your circle of friends. When the time is right, tell them your spiritual story.

49. Background: Kevin is a 32 year old male from China. He came to the U.S. in 2002 when he was 29. He had an M.A. when he entered the U.S. in Texas to study for his Ph.D. in Electrical Engineering. He has no plans to become a U.S. citizen.

Conversion: Kevin was an atheist in China, but when he got here he got a Bible and started reading. He had lots of questions about Christianity. Though an atheist, he had difficulty believing that there was nothing after death. The Bible and Christianity provided him with the answers he was looking for. Within a couple of months, Kevin became a Christian.

Advice: When asked what advice he had for church leaders who want to work effectively with people who were new to the U.S., Kevin said that giving them a free Bible was important. Most Chinese are very private, Kevin explained, so don't intrude into personal areas. Wait until they open up.

50. Background: Li is a 31 year old female from China who came to the U.S. in 2003 when she was 28. She came to Texas with her husband who came to study. Li has a BA in accounting. She has not had an opportunity to continue her education and has no plans to become a U.S. citizen.

Conversion: In China, Li was an atheist, but became a Christian in a little over a year following the lead of her husband who became a Christian. Watching his spiritual growth convinced her that Christianity was right.

Advice: When asked what advice she had for church leaders who want to reach out to immigrants, Li said to be warm hearted. Be friends and stay in their lives. Invite them to church. Eat together. Help with whatever material issues need attention. Give new arrivals time to watch, learn and get comfortable. Give God time to work.

Summary

These 50 interviewees represent seven different cultural groups (either Asian or Latino) and several different religious backgrounds. Each of the 50 was converted to a conservative protestant expression of the Christian faith after leaving their home culture to start a new life in America. Some were converted soon after immigration. A few were converted before they even arrived in the U.S. And some were not converted for years. But all were converted. Why? There were many different reasons. You noticed, no doubt, that there were a number of recurring themes. In Chapter 4 we will analyze what the interviewees told us in more detail, looking for the themes that are present.

Chapter 4

Profile Data:
Analysis and Observations

Even a cursory reading of these profiles reveals a number of recurring themes and items of special interest that merit specific attention.

Any analysis of qualitative data such as this is subjective and another researcher may see alternative categories to include in his or her analysis. I have attempted to offset this subjective factor by including as many specific categories as present themselves in the profiles.

The interview responses are divided into three broad categories:

1. life issues or felt needs that prompted interviewees to:
   A. seek assistance, or
   B. examine or reevaluate their existing spiritual state,
(Note: not all interviewees shared with us things that would fall under this first category.)
2. things Christians did that aided or promoted a positive response and led to the conversion experience,
3. advice interviewees had for church leaders who want to engage in effective outreach to immigrants.

Each of those three categories then contains a number of sub-categories that represent specific responses and/or advice.

Life Issues or Felt Needs

Under category 1: *Life issues or felt needs that prompted interviewees to: seek assistance, or examine or reevaluate their existing spiritual state*, the following sub-categories were mentioned by interviewees. The order of the list reflects the number of times the item was mentioned. The number of interviewees who mentioned each item is noted. Interviewees felt:

1. confused, hurt, empty or alone: 6
2. the stress of personal or family illness or issues: 4
3. a need for God's presence in their lives: 3
4. the need to learn English and American culture: 2
5. the need for truth and spiritual guidance offered in the Bible: 2
6. a desire for clarity in life, a need to understand: 2
7. an awareness of spiritual needs that were not being met: 1
8. the need to better themselves: 1
9. the need to belong to something (inclusion in a group): 1
10. a need for change: 1
11. a growing interest in spiritual things: 1
12. a lack of purpose or direction in life: 1

Notice the first half of the list:

1. people who felt hurting, confused, empty or alone,
2. people who were experiencing personal or family illness or issues,
3. those who were feeling a need for God's presence in their lives,

4. those who felt a need to learn English and American culture,
5. those who the need for truth and spiritual guidance offered in the Bible,
6. those who felt a need for some truth, guidance, clarity and understanding in their lives.

Noticing these first six items does not diminish the importance of the other six items mentioned by our interviewees. But these are the feelings and experiences that came up most often during our interviews. Some of them represent different expressions of similar needs. In thinking about how to serve the needs of an immigrant community, church leaders would do well to keep in mind the kind of needs and issues that led to conversion for many of the people in this study.

Things Christians Did

Under category 2: *Things Christians did that aided or promoted a positive response and led to the conversion experience*, the following sub-categories were mentioned by interviewees. They are listed in the order they were mentioned most often and the number of interviewees who mentioned each item is noted. Christians:

1. were loving, kind, friendly, and willing to help: 13
2. demonstrated Christianity by their actions: 9
3. did not push for a quick response, gave people time to watch, listen and learn: 9
4. made use of small group Bible studies/discussions: 9
5. provided teaching that was biblical in its source and content: 8
6. helped with physical needs—bills, food, transportation, housing, medical, and so forth: 5
7. invited them to church: 5

8. helped them focus on spiritual things and value God's presence in their lives: 4
9. offered programs for teaching English and American culture: 4
10. provided teaching that was relevant to life: 3
11. provided comfort and encouragement during times of difficulty: 2
12. invited them to fellowships and activities: 2
13. prayed for them: 2
14. developed a relationship with them: 1
15. spent time with them just being friends: 1
16. studied the Bible in a person's own language: 1

Let's look more closely at the seven items mentioned most often (arranged by the number of times they were mentioned by our interviewees). The things mentioned most often by our interviewees that Christians did that aided or promoted a positive response and led to the conversion experience, included:

1. being loving, kind, friendly, and willing to help,
2. demonstrating their faith through their actions,
3. not pushing for a quick response, giving people time to watch, listen and learn
4. making use of small group Bible studies/discussions
5. providing teaching that was biblical in its source and content
6. helping with physical needs—bills, food, transportation, housing, medical, and so forth
7. inviting them to church

As with the previous list, making special mention of these seven items in no way diminishes the importance of the other items mentioned by the people we interviewed. However, these seven kept popping up in interview after interview, making them worth special notice.

Christians impressed immigrants most by their friendliness, kindness, and loving behavior that was apparent in their willingness to help people they did not know without expecting anything in return. This kind of behavior is strange to people from cultures where Christianity is not the predominant religion. In many other cultures, strangers are often tolerated or ignored. When people from those kinds of cultures come to America and find a group of people who are kind, friendly and helpful to strangers they are surprised and curious as to the motivation for that kind of behavior. Their curiosity provides believers with opportunities to witness and teach.

Another comment that we heard often had to do with believers who demonstrated their faith through the things they did for immigrants. Being kind and friendly, loving and helpful is essentially the same as demonstrating one's faith by the way one lives. But since some of our interviewees were very specific about Christians demonstrating their faith through their actions, the idea deserves specific mention. Immigrants became aware that they were seeing Christianity being demonstrated for them, helping them understand in a very concrete way what the Christian faith is about. They saw Christianity before anyone explained it to them. When they heard it explained to them, it was easier to understand because they had already seen an example of it. There is no preaching or teaching that is as powerful as the living of the Christian life.

A third comment we heard often as immigrants told us their conversion stories was that the Christians with whom they had contact did not push them for a quick response to the Gospel. They were patient, giving people a chance to see and hear, to think and decide. Many of the immigrants we interviewed were former Catholics. Catholicism was their traditional family religion. In most non-Western cultures, such as Latino cultures, family traditions are strong and not easily replaced with something new. Change comes slowly.

A number of the people we interviewed had come from non-religious families. For them it was not a matter of replacing a long standing religious tradition, but becoming a person of faith for the first time. Again, not something that usually happens very quickly.

Some believers are taught to make a short, powerful presentation of the Gospel and expect and push for a quick response. After all, eternity hangs in the balance! That is a very Western way of thinking about things. But the Gospel is not Western and neither are the immigrants who are coming here from other cultures. They do not embrace new ways quickly or easily. Many of them come from cultures considerably older than our own, cultures rooted in ancient wisdom and centuries of experience. Immigrants from those cultures will take a wait and see attitude for things that are new and different—which is what Christianity is to them, new and different.

In our evangelistic zeal, justified and appropriate as it is, we need to learn to slow down and let people think. They need to observe, sometimes for a long time, to see if this Christian kindness and love is real or not. When they are convinced, they will respond. The best thing we can do is be patient, continue to be friends, and invite them to participate as often and much as they are willing.

The fourth comment that we heard often had to do with the use of small group Bible discussions. There are three key ideas here: small group, Bible and discussion.

Small groups have a distinct nature and feel about them. The intimacy and informal atmosphere of prayer and Bible discussions that occur in someone's home allow people to relax and open up, asking and answering questions that would never come up in a larger group in a more formal setting. Anyone who has participated in small groups on a regular basis for a time knows this and appreciates the value of small groups for outreach as well as nurturing. A number of our interviewees confirmed this by suggesting that small groups had been instrumental in their conversion. Churches who are not yet using small groups are failing to make use of a very effective tool for evangelism and spiritual formation.

The heart of a small group discussion must be the Bible. There must be time for sharing and prayers, but this must be regulated so adequate time is available for Bible discussions. The topics for discussion must grow out of or be directed back to the Bible, for the Bible is God's primary communication to us and God must be allowed to speak through the Scriptures. Whether we begin with a Bible verse and consider how it applies to our lives, or whether we begin with a life question and go to the Scriptures to see what God has to say regarding that issue, the Bible must be integral to the gathering.

Finally, the key to successful small group Bible discussions is *discussion.* Not a lecture, but a guided discussion. *Guided* is important because if a knowledgeable guide is not leading and assisting the discussion it deteriorates into a session of shared ignorance. Uninformed opinions are not very useful. But in our contemporary society neither is a lecture. People want to discuss not be told. They want to share their thinking and raise questions for discussion. A good small group discussion group leader knows how to lead a discussion that will not deteriorate, on the one hand, into a session of shared ignorance or, on the other hand, into a boring lecture. He or she will know how to balance his or her input of information with the ebb and flow of a thoughtful discussion that will engage, inform and enlighten the members of the group, keeping them interested, learning and returning.

A fifth recurring theme of our interviews was the importance of Bible teaching. Relevance is important. A number of people mentioned relevance. But an important point for many of our interviewees was teaching that is biblical, because biblical teaching is authoritative. Our secular pluralistic society is filled with relativistic opinions on just about everything. At some point people realize that a relativistic life without authoritative boundaries is a life without structure, direction and purpose. Life is lived best when it is lived within a context of moral absolutes and divine purpose—a life lived in relationship with God. It is the Bible that shows us how to do this, that provides us with the guidance we need to excel as human beings.

Whether or not individuals articulate their deep spiritual longings in terms of biblical authority, many of them understand that biblical teaching is essential if their deepest needs are to be met. They want a connection with God and feel the Bible provides them with what they need. That is why they want spiritually authoritative teaching.

If biblical teaching is to be meaningful, however, it must also be relevant to life. When our interviewees referred to biblical teaching they were not thinking of theological details that are of interest, for the most part, only to theologians. Biblical teaching that is helpful is relevant. It has to do with how to live a better life. This is the kind of teaching that characterized Jesus' ministry and which will characterize ours if we are making a difference in people's lives.

The sixth recurring theme of our interviews had to do with Christians assisting immigrants with their often challenging physical circumstances—helping financially with their various expenses, providing transportation, food, assistance with complex medical and educational systems, and so forth.

Over the centuries some believers have failed to understand the holistic nature of the Christian message. Ultimately the Good News about Jesus has to do with the salvation of the soul. Yet, throughout the Scriptures, Old Testament and New, God is constantly aware of, concerned about, and involved in the physical side of his children's lives. God created us as physical beings. In the incarnation he became one himself. The Mosaic Covenant contained numerous laws which safeguarded the physical needs of human beings. During Jesus' ministry, he demonstrated over and over again not only a willingness but a determination to assist people with their physical concerns.

A message about God's love delivered by people of means to individuals in physical despair seems strangely incongruous if it is not accompanied by demonstrations of love designed to ease the burdens of life. The message, *God loves you and we "love" you but all we're going to do for you is teach you and baptize you,* doesn't quite add up, does it?

Benevolence and missions go hand-in-hand. We budget them separately, but they are not really separate. More of our resources (financial and human) need to be spent on helping people. Hungry people need to be fed. Sick people need to be taken to the doctor. People who are new to this culture and unfamiliar with our medical system and how it works will need help understanding and getting comfortable with a simple thing like going to the clinic. To new immigrants, taking a sick child to the doctor or enrolling a child in school, or going to a government office to fill out more forms can be confusing and even traumatic. Deposits that must be paid in advance for rent and utilities can exhaust a family's reserves leaving them without sufficient resources until a job is secured and a paycheck is received. Should we not be willing to help with these kinds of needs?

The seventh recurring item among the things that Christians did to aid or promote a positive response that led to the conversion of many immigrants was simply to invite them to church. Often is it the obvious that is overlooked. People who are new to our culture, especially if they come from non-Western cultures as most immigrants to the U.S. do, are not going to show up at church one Sunday and, in effect, say, *OK, here we are. We have come to see what you people are all about.* Even if they are curious, even if they are already interested, the vast majority will not visit a church they are not already a member of without a specific invitation. Many, however, will come to a worship assembly or fellowship if they are invited, even if they are unaware of a spiritual need or interest. Many will come simply because someone invited them, and once there, they will be intrigued by the friendly people and helpful nature of the topics presented. Of course it helps if the "someone" who invites them has been friendly and helpful already.

The immigrants we interviewed told us about many things believers did that played a positive role in their eventual conversion experience. As I counted, our 50 interviewees mentioned about sixteen specific things. I have highlighted seven of them. In the simplest terms, what we learned was that all the people we interviewed became Christians because someone took an interest in them. Someone cared enough to help them, to be a friend, and to find some way to bring Christ into the relationship.

Advice from Immigrants for Church Leaders

Under category 3, *advice interviewees had for church leaders who want to engage in effective outreach to immigrants*, the individuals we spoke with gave advice in twenty-two different areas. Again, the order of the list reflects the order of importance, or the number of times that piece of advice was offered.

Church leaders need to:

1. get to know the people; love them, be kind, be friends: 14
2. help immigrants with their physical needs: 11
3. learn the culture of the people with whom you wish to work so you can understand how they think: 7
4. demonstrate Christian love—let the people see God working in your life: 6
5. know not to push for quick conversion decisions: 6
6. make use of small groups for Bible discussions: 6

7. respect the beliefs of immigrants and not be critical: 5
8. help people first and wait until later to teach them: 3
9. be patient: 3
10. provide avenues for immigrants to learn English and American culture: 3
11. utilize Spanish radio to reach Latino communities: 3
12. provide lots of opportunities for fellowship and involvement: 2
13. reach the teens and children of immigrants with activities and teaching: 2
14. be proactive, inviting immigrants to church and other activities: 2
15. provide biblical teaching: 2
16. make use of immigrant networks to make contacts within the immigrant community: 1
17. be open so immigrants can get to know them: 1
18. avoid asking for money: 1
19. pray a lot, asking for the Holy Spirit to lead: 1
20. find ways to connect the Gospel to the immigrant's culture: 1
21. give Bibles to people who don't have one: 1
22. respect people's privacy: 1

It may be helpful to remember that in surveys designed to gather quantitative data researchers design questions with pre-selected answers (A. B. C. D.) or pre-selected categories for respondents to measure (on a scale of 1 to 5). However, our interviews were designed to produce qualitative data, that is, information given to us by the interviewees without us suggesting possible answers. The lists produced from analyzing the data reflect the original and personal thinking of the people we interviewed. This list of 22 pieces of advice is what the 50 immigrants we interviewed felt church leaders ought to know about working with immigrants. Let's think a little more closely about the first six in the list.

1. *Get to know the people; love them, be kind, be friends.* Why would so many immigrants who have been converted feel the need to advise church leaders about getting to know immigrants (personally) and being kind and friendly to them? Could it be that being in a cultural environment they do not fully understand, and perhaps separated from their larger family and community of friends, feeling confused and perhaps isolated and vulnerable, that friendship is very important to them? Since most immigrants to the U.S. are from non-Western cultures, they are from cultures that place a high value (much higher than we do) on family and friends, on being part of a community, part of a group. They value friendship and need to feel that people know them and care about them.

I suspect that immigrants are telling us this because of the deep significance they place on friendship and kindness. They know the impact kindness and friendship had on them and know how much it will impact others. They know what a lonely process immigration is and how important friendship is. And they know that this may not come as easily for Americans (as independent and individualistic as we are) as it comes for people who are more interdependent, more group oriented. It's not that Americans are unfriendly, or unkind. It is simply that as independent, individualistic Americans we do not *need* other people as much or as deeply as people from other cultural groups. Immigrants may not understand why this is true, but I believe they seem to sense it. So they are encouraging us to do what they need us to do—reach out to them in a friendly, caring way.

2. *Help immigrants with their physical needs.* The obvious question, again, is, why would so many of the people we interviewed want to advise church leaders to help immigrants with their physical needs? Perhaps it is because so many of them lived for a time without the ability to adequately meet their or their family's needs. Many

96

immigrants arrive here with empty pockets. Getting here took all they had. There are different forms of public assistance, but it takes time to get and often the process for getting it—government buildings, lines, forms—can be confusing, intimidating or even overwhelming.

Perhaps many of the people we interviewed were the fortunate ones who received some kind of help from a group of caring Christians and they know how deeply it moved them. Perhaps they understand how such demonstrations of Christian love can lead one to explore this thing called Christianity.

Of course, there are always those unscrupulous people who are making the rounds and milking the "system" for all it's worth. It's helpful to have some kind of screening or referral system to weed out the freeloaders. But some will get though and some of our scarce resources will go to people who don't really deserve them. Which is worse: to be taken advantage of, or to refuse to help truly needy people?

3. *Learn the culture of the people with whom you wish to work so you can understand how they think.* Why should I learn the culture of El Salvador or Honduras, of the Dominican Republic or China, of Pakistan or the Philippines? If people from those countries want to make America their home they should learn American culture.

Yes, they should. And they will—eventually. But it takes time. And in the meantime you want to be leading them to Christ. To do that effectively you need to understand who they are. You need to understand their culture so you can understand their way of thinking about life, so you can share the story of Jesus with them in a way that makes sense to them. That's called *contextualization*. You don't change the Gospel, but you change the way you present it. Paul practiced contextualization in his ministry and he recommended it as a necessary tool for effective proclamation. When he wrote to the believers in Corinth he said:

97

> *When I am with the Jews, I become one of them so that I can bring them to Christ. When I am with those who follow the Jewish laws, I do the same, even though I am not subject to the law, so that I can bring them to Christ. When I am with the Gentiles who do not have the Jewish law, I fit in with them as much as I can. In this way, I gain their confidence and bring them to Christ. But I do not discard the law of God; I obey the law of Christ.*
>
> *When I am with those who are oppressed, I share their oppression so that I might bring them to Christ. Yes, I try to find common ground with everyone so that I might bring them to Christ. I do all this to spread the Good News, and in doing so I enjoy its blessings,* (1 Cor 9:20-23).

We can see what Paul is talking about when we compare his sermon in Acts 13 with his sermon in Acts 17. Each sermon was preached to a different audience, one Jewish, one Greek. While both sermons are a presentation of the Good News, each is a very different presentation. Paul contextualized his message.

To be able to do this effectively Paul had to understand both Jewish and Greek perspectives on life. Since Paul was Jewish, understanding a Jewish perspective was not difficult. Understanding a Greek perspective, however, especially a group of educated philosophers like those in Athens, required Paul to spend some time learning about Greeks and Greeks philosophers. In other words, Paul had to spend some time learning a culture other than his own. We need to do the same.

4. *Demonstrate Christian love—let the people see God working in your life.* This piece of advice is related to point number two, helping with physical needs. But the immigrants we interviewed had an additional quality in mind. They were talking about living in such a way that God's love could be seen in the lives of his people. This means living lives of love that touch people in many different ways: visiting them when they are sick, comforting them when they hurt, encouraging them when they are down,

celebrating with them when they are happy. It means being a kind, joyous, patient, caring, peaceful, confident, humble, person—the kind of person others enjoy being around and to whom others will go when they need help.

None of our interviewees put their thoughts in exactly these words, but this is what I believe they were talking about. Somewhere along the way they had encountered a Barnabas kind of person and they liked it. They sensed God living in and working through that person and they recognize what a powerful influence that kind of person can have on others. So they are advising church leaders to be those kinds of people—people in whom God lives and through whom God works to touch the lives of people who do not yet know him.

5. *Provided teaching that is biblical in its source and content.* As noted earlier, immigrants want authoritative biblical teaching. They want to be guided by God in their daily lives. But here is the difficult part: *authoritative, biblical teaching for people of other cultures must not be ethnocentric, monocultural, Anglo-perspective teaching that makes perfectly good sense to us but often leaves people from other cultures feeling like their needs are not being understood or addressed.*

Christianity is not a monocultural faith, and biblical interpretation and application must be cross-cultural and multiethnic if it is to be useful in our multiethnic society, to say nothing of the larger global village we call Earth. God designed Christianity to have meaning in every cultural context. That's what Paul was talking about when he spoke to the believers in Corinth about his practice of contextualizing the message about Jesus (1 Cor. 9:20-23).

What it boils down to is this: there is more than one way to interpret and apply the Bible. Anglo-Americans think like Anglo-Americans, not like Chinese, Indians, Africans, Mexicans, or Brazilians. The way we interpret and apply the Bible works for us. It meets our needs and fits our

99

ways of thinking and doing. But our ways of thinking and doing do not necessarily work for people of other cultures—whether they still live in those cultures or have come here to live in America.

We need to understand that authoritative biblical teaching does not mean Anglo-American interpretation and application. The eternal truths of God's authoritative Word must be applied in culturally appropriate ways so that Christianity comes alive for every ethnic group. Can an Anglo provide that kind of teaching? Some can. Others cannot. It depends on how much training one has in cross-cultural communication and contextualization and how much one understands about the ethnic group in question. Obviously the best way to provide authoritative biblical teaching for a given ethnic group is to find someone of that ethnic group to minister to them.

6. *Make use of small groups for Bible discussions.* As noted already, people prefer to discuss rather than merely listen. They also prefer the relaxed intimacy of sitting in someone's living room or family room, or around the dining table while discussing very important and personal matters such as faith and spiritual needs. A number of the people we interviewed spoke of Christians spending time with them as friends. One lady mentioned eating together. Others spoke often of regular fellowship in people's homes.

If you are not using your home for small group discussions, let me encourage you to begin. There's lots of really good small group discussion guides available in most Christian book stores. Buy several. Read them. Find one you really like and invite some of your friends from church AND (and this is the most important part) some of your neighbors or friends who are not Christians to your home for a Bible *discussion.* A group of eight to ten works best, split evenly, if possible, between Christians and non-Christians.

Have everyone sit in some approximation of a circle and ask a provocative opening question that has something to do with a text that you'd eventually like to discuss. For instance, if your text is 2 Corinthians 4:16-18, you could begin by saying, "Some people tend to live in the past, some tend to live in the present, to live for the moment. Others maintain a constant focus on the future. Given those three options, how would you characterize your orientation—past, present or future?" Follow up question might be, "What are the strengths and weaknesses of each orientation?"

Let everyone talk for a while and then read your text and ask someone what they think about it. You should select a text that is practical and that does not need a lot of historical background information in order to understand. Keep it simple and practical so that people with no Bible background can participate.

Go with the flow. Don't worry about staying on a track and accomplishing a specific purpose. The purpose is to get everyone talking comfortably about spiritual matters. It's not that hard, really. Be patient. Smile a lot. Nod a lot.

After an hour suggest that it has been an interesting discussion and ask if everyone would come back next week and do it again. Then invite everyone to help themselves to some snacks and visit for a while. Don't put out a fancy spread. Keep it simple, easy and inexpensive. Use paper plates and cups.

The first few weeks may be kind of bumpy, but keep going. The group may shrink and grow, participants may change. But eventually a group will form and develop a kind of a personality. That's when it gets interesting and really helpful. The Lord uses groups like that. Give him one to work with.

Summary

In analyzing the data gathered from our interviews, the material falls into three broad categories:
1. life issues or felt needs that prompted interviewees to:

A. seek assistance, or

B. examine or reevaluate their existing spiritual state,

2. things Christians did that aided or promoted a positive response and led to the conversion experience,

3. advice interviewees had for church leaders who want to engage in effective outreach to immigrants.

I believe that it is fair to say that some immigrants were experiencing challenges in their lives (some directly related to immigration and others not at all related) that generated an openness to spiritual things. Those who did not mention such challenges may not have been consciously aware of internal conflicts that also made them open to spiritual concerns. All of them, however, were open and all of them were converted.

Most of them had something to say about the kindness of believers who cared about them. The personal relationship made all the difference. Many of our interviewees referred to Bible studies that impacted them and led to a change. There is no doubt about that. But even those studies occurred in the context of someone who cared enough to make an effort, to spend time, to help, to teach. The personal touch was there, even if it did not stand out to everyone we interviewed. Friends studied the Scriptures together and God used that relationship to change a life. That's the way it works. People impact people through relationships.

When the people we interviewed were given a chance to give some advice to church leaders about effective outreach among immigrants, most of their advice had something to do with a loving, kind, helpful relationship that will eventually change lives.

In the next chapter, immigrants who minister to immigrants will provide some important insights on effective outreach and ministry among people who are new to this country.

Chapter 5

Immigrants Who Minister
To Immigrants

One of the best sources of information on how to effectively reach immigrant communities with the Gospel and how to build a congregation of *ethnically-other* believers who can serve their growing communities is the ministers who are themselves members of those immigrant communities and who work each day with foreign-born U.S. residents. This chapter will be a report of the information gathered in interviews with six ministers who immigrated to this country and who now serve as ministers in the Lord's church. Four of them serve churches made up of people from various Latino cultures, two serve churches made up of people from Asian cultures. The interview guide used in our conversations with these ministers is reproduced in Appendix B.

Interview Profiles[1]

1. Background: Henry was born in Colombia. He was raised a Catholic and attended a Catholic high school where the curriculum included some very basic Bible lessons. Henry's aunt answered an ad that missionaries in Guatemala had placed in a Bogotá newspaper offering a free Bible correspondence course. She received her first lesson but did not have a Bible. Henry had a New Testament from his high school classes so he and his aunt began studying the Bible together using his New Testament. In 1969, Henry, along with his aunt, was converted to a conservative protestant expression of the Christian faith.

As he matured, Henry knew he wanted to spend his life in service to the Lord, so in 1975 he came to the U.S. to study for the ministry. After graduating from an intensive two-year program, Henry returned to Colombia where he served a church not far from Bogotá.

In 1986, Henry was contacted by a Latino church in Dallas, Texas, that invited him to come and serve as their minister. Henry accepted the invitation and came to Texas, serving that church for nearly 15 years. Henry has been in full-time ministry for over 30 years.

Ministry Insights: When asked, what is the most challenging aspect of ministry among Latinos, Henry explained that *there are two: 1) developing leaders and, 2) integration issues.*

As far as leadership is concerned, Henry explained that *leadership in Latino churches tends to be one extreme or*

---

[1] In the process of synthesizing and reporting the information from these interviews, I have taken the liberty of explaining what an individual meant by a particular insight or piece of advice, or I have expanded on what he said. I have not changed anyone's comments, but have explained and elaborated. The *Background* sections are presented in brief biographical form. In the *Ministry Insights* and *Advice* sections, the interviewees comments are in italic, my comments are in regular type.

the other: either nonexistent or authoritarian. In researching this phenomenon, I have discovered that since most Latino believers are from Mexico, the leadership challenges have to do with sociocultural issues in Mexico. In much of Mexico's culture, some researchers suggest, it is simply not acceptable to assert oneself as one must do to be a leader. There are two reasons for this. First, through centuries of political domination and outright oppression, Mexicans have learned to maintain a low profile and be submissive. Second, those who do attempt to assert themselves are often criticized for their apparent lack of humility and presumption of authority. Thus, it is challenging to find a Mexican male who is willing to think in terms of leadership. [Note, not all Mexicans would agree with this cultural assessment.]

Henry went on to explain, *Because of a general lack of experienced Latino leaders to provide a healthy, acceptable role model of effective leadership, those who do attempt leadership, often tend to be authoritarian in their manner and approach.* I have experienced this myself in working with Latinos. Often men who are looked to as leaders are unwilling to accept the responsibility of leadership. Without leadership it is difficult for Latino churches to grow beyond dependency on Anglo churches, which creates low spiritual self-esteem and a number of related spiritual problems.

As for integration with Anglo believers, Henry explained *that many Latinos remain uneasy about integration with Anglos.* Again, in researching this tendency I discovered that many Latinos (especially first generation Latinos) do not want to be assimilated into mainstream Anglo culture. Their preference for retaining their own cultural identity, combined with being "uncomfortable" around Anglos makes it a challenge to achieve and sustain meaningful integration between some Latinos and Anglos.

For most Latinos, it is not that they dislike Anglos. It is a cultural response. Most Latinos do not understand why

Anglos are the way we are. (Most Anglos don't know why we are the way we are!) We don't think or act like Latinos and Latinos are uncomfortable around us. This is perfectly normal in any cross-cultural encounter until the different ethnic groups get to know each other. Lots of Anglos are uncomfortable around Latinos when they (the Anglos) find themselves in the minority. A couple of lone Anglos in a large group of Latinos can feel just as uncomfortable as a couple of Latinos feel in a large group of Anglos. It's a normal reaction. The challenge is getting Latinos and Anglos together often enough, long enough in a relaxed atmosphere so they can get comfortable with one another.

When Henry was asked, what outreach methods work best with Latinos, Henry said *small Bible discussion groups that meet weekly in people's homes.* This should not be surprising since many of our interviewees referred to the importance of small groups in their own conversion or advised church leaders to make use of small groups in outreach efforts to immigrants. Why are small groups so effective with immigrants? Because small groups in people's homes provide a relaxed setting that is not culturally intimidating. Sitting and discussing issues with a small group of friends is a familiar occurrence. People from all cultures sit around with friends and discuss things. So even in a larger cultural context that may be foreign, a small group meeting informally in someone's home feels familiar. It's a comfortable place to talk, to express one's feelings and thoughts, to ask questions, to hear new ideas, to hear someone's story about how their life has been impacted in a positive way by their relationship with Jesus.

For most people, a small group discussion in the relaxed atmosphere of a friend's home is a safe, inviting place to be.

When Henry was asked, what is an effective way of nurturing Latino believers, Henry explained that *in addition to small groups, which are effective for nurturing as well as for evangelism, I am experimenting with producing a series of ten minute spiritual formation DVDs.* With his cameraman in tow, Henry goes to different locations around the city which might have a visual tie-in with an idea he wants to present from the Bible. In that setting he will read the text and talk briefly about it, spending most of his time on meaningful, helpful application. His themes are positive "how to live better" themes. In an editing session, Henry adds some introduction and background music and whatever graphics are helpful. The final product is a ten minute devotional DVD to copy and give out to members for that week's meditation moment.

The whole idea is still in the experimental stages, but Henry hopes for a good result. With Latinos or Anglos, it is challenging to get them to slow down and think about God during a busy week. Providing them with an interesting and inspirational meditation guide may be as motivational as it is helpful. The key to spiritual formation is to get people to slow down and spend time with God.

Advice: When asked what advice he had for church leaders who want to begin a multiethnic church, Henry had three suggestions.

1. *Leaders need to devote plenty of time to learning and understanding the cultural group they are interested in working with,*

2. *Leaders need to communicate with and get a commitment from the whole church to be involved in and dedicated to the challenge of being a multiethnic church,*

3. *Leaders need to be open to learning from the new cultural group.*

Let's think for a moment about what Henry has said.

1. *Leaders need to devote plenty of time to learning and understanding the cultural group they are interested in working with.* A number of our interviewees made this same point. Well-intentioned or not, if you don't understand the culture of the people with whom you want to share the Good

107

News, you're probably not going to do a very good job of it. You can't communicate effectively with people you don't understand.

How can leaders get to know the culture of another group of people? There are three ways. First, buy some books and read them. There are books out there on virtually every cultural group on the planet. There are lots of books written about the major cultural groups, such as Latinos. The big bookstore chains will have books on their shelves about other cultures. If you go online to a bookseller and type in a subject search for, let's say, Latino culture, dozens of books will come up. Buy several and read them.

Second, find a couple that are part of the ethnic group you want to understand and spend time getting to know them. Invite them over for dinner. Develop a friendship. After a few months, when the friendship is strong, show them some of the books you have read. Ask them some questions. Mostly, just spend time with them, eating, laughing, talking, thinking, just being friends. You will learn a great deal, not only about them as people, but about them as members of an ethnic group.

Third, go out into the neighborhoods where people of the ethnic group you want to work with eat, shop and otherwise live their lives. Interact with them. Make friends. Talk with them. Discover what issues concern them. What concerns do they have about their children? What concerns do they have about education, health care, politics? What is it like to be them? When you begin to have some insights into what their lives are like, then you begin to understand how to help them, how to bring Jesus into their lives in meaningful ways.

2. *Leaders need to communicate with and get a commitment from the whole church to be involved in and dedicated to the challenge of being a multiethnic church.* Becoming a multiethnic church involves much more than simply hiring an ethnic minister, giving him a room in which to have a

worship assembly in a different language, and then sitting back to see how many of those people show up.

A multiethnic church is not simply an Anglo body of believers that grows another appendage somewhere that is then basically ignored by the rest of the body. On more than one occasion I have visited Anglo "multiethnic" churches and asked people where the Latinos (or some other ethnic group) met only to be met by bewildered expressions of confusion and uncertainty. "We have Mexicans meeting here?" Or, "Oh, yeah, the Mexicans. Let's see, where are they?"

The decision to become a multiethnic church is more than an executive decision involving facility usage. The decision to become a multiethnic church involves an awareness and a sincere concern on the part of the whole church that there is a group of people in the community with cultural needs different from their own, a group of people that each of them needs to be concerned about, to pray about, to learn about, and to be willing to serve in any way they can.

It can take as much as one year of regular, intentional teaching, praying, research, planning, and preparation to get a church ready to become a multiethnic church. A well-trained minister who is himself a member of the ethnic group you want to reach should be hired as much as a year in advance to lead the research and planning, and to help encourage the church to embrace the idea and plan for cross-cultural outreach and ministry. Only when the whole church is involved in the planning, the preparation, the funding and the implementation will the effort be as successful as it can be.

3. *Leaders need to be open to learning from the new cultural group.* Immigrants may be new to this country. They may not fully understand us or our culture. But that does not mean that they have no wisdom or useful insights to offer. It does not mean that they are not capable of significant

contributions. They are smart, tenacious, hardworking people who can make an important difference in a local church if given a voice.

Leaders need to spend a lot of time listening to ethnically-other people. They bring a perspective that is often totally lacking on our part. They see things about us and our culture that we don't see. Listen to them.

2. Background: Sixto is from El Salvador. For a period of time he lived with his father in Honduras. Because of political unrest Honduras became a dangerous place to live, so Sixto and his father moved back to El Salvador. However, when war came to El Salvador as well, it was necessary to escape. Over eighty thousand people died in the conflict in El Salvador.

During those difficult times, life was a challenge and Sixto's father was searching for meaning and truth. The Catholic church seemed unable to meet his needs. Sixto's father eventually found a conservative protestant expression of the Christian faith that made sense to him. He taught Sixto what he had learned. Sixto began his spiritual journey in El Salvador and continued it during his immigration to the U.S. in 1982. Eventually Sixto, as his father had, embraced a conservative protestant form of Christianity and knew he wanted to serve his Lord as a minister. He has been a minister to his fellow Latinos for sixteen years.

Ministry Insights: When asked, what is the most challenging aspect of ministry to Latinos, Sixto explained that *many Latinos are very interested in recreational activities, especially on weekends. Sports consume a lot of their time, as do gatherings with family and friends. Weekends can be so full of other activities that finding time for spiritual pursuits can be challenging.*

As Sixto shared this insight with me, I thought about how true this is for most people. Leisure time is quickly filled with activities designed to relax and distract. Whether people do this consciously, knowing their intention is to distract themselves from matters that require serious and sometimes uncomfortable contemplation, or unconsciously, without realizing why they are filling their time with distracting activities, the result is the same: people are too busy to give due consideration to spiritual matters.

When asked, what is the most effective outreach method when working with Latinos, Sixto explained that *friendship evangelism works best.* I believe this is true for all people. People are most comfortable talking about important matters with friends or family, with people they know and trust. Nearly everyone knows someone who is not a Christian. The newer the Christian, the more non-Christian people he or she will know. New believers need to be encouraged to share their new faith and new spiritual life with their friends. Keeping new believers involved in a small group provides them with a place to bring their friends and family to introduce them to Christianity in a relaxed, casual manner.

When asked, what nurturing or ministry methods work best with Latinos, Sixto explained that *there are two elements that he believes are essential. One is teaching people to develop a deep relationship with God. Too many Christians know something about God, but do not really know God. The key to spiritual formation is for each Christian to develop a deep relationship with God and allow God, through his Spirit to guide and form each believer.*

The second essential for nurturing is creating an atmosphere where people can express their concerns and challenges, their worries and weaknesses, without the fear of criticism or rejection. Believers must be free to ask, to complain, to confess, and know they will be loved and accepted as they struggle with the issues of life. In that kind of supportive atmosphere spiritual growth can occur.

Advice: When asked, what advice would you give to church leaders who want to begin multiethnic churches, Sixto said

111

that *the most important thing was to create within the whole church an atmosphere where Anglos and non-Anglos can interact safely, without the fear of compromising their ethnic identity. There can be no cultural domination. People must be allowed to be who they are—culturally speaking.*

All believers must grow and change so their lives reflect God's image and glory. None of us is yet who we ought to be. Growth and change (from more sinful to less sinful) is the goal of Christian living. But the need to change does not include the need to change one's cultural and ethnic identity. Becoming a Christian or becoming a better Christian does not mean becoming an Anglo. God loves all ethnic groups. He loves Latinos and Asians and Africans and Anglos and everybody else. Latinos don't have to become Asian, Anglos don't have to become African. Everyone can remain (ethnically) who they are as long as they are allowing the Holy Spirit to help them become better people. Church leaders need to create an atmosphere within the local body of Christ where ethnic identity is safe and secure.

3. Background: Bob is from Taiwan. Bob's parents were Christians who established an orphanage in Taiwan. Bob was raised in a family of deep faith and service to God and to people. At twelve years old, Bob gave his life to the Lord and was baptized. In 1983, at twenty-four years old, after completing university and serving in the military for two years, Bob came to the U.S. to complete graduate school. He earned an M.A. in Statistics from Louisiana State University. While in graduate school he decided that he wanted to spend his life in ministry to others. Bob has been in ministry now for 28 years and is working on a Doctor of Ministry degree. Bob ministers to mostly Chinese from mainland China and from Taiwan.
Ministry Insights: When asked, what is the most challenging aspect of working with the Chinese, Bob

explained that *the answer depends on which subgroup is being considered. Mainland Chinese are different from Taiwanese.* When thinking in terms of mainland Chinese, Bob explained *that after the Cultural Revolution in China the society had little in the way of values; they had no spiritual beliefs. They are very rational, very philosophically and scientifically oriented. But spiritually they are empty. Many of them are searching for something to fill the spiritual void in their lives, but they tend to evaluate everything from their rational, scientific perspective. So in working with them the challenge is to present Christianity in a rational way that is compatible with a scientific orientation.*

Taiwanese people present a different challenge. The Taiwanese have a very strong secular orientation. They are very materialistic and not easily interested in spiritual matters. Their spiritual indifference can be a challenge to overcome.

When asked, what method of outreach is most effective with Chinese people, Bob said, *"like people reach like people."* He was referring to a basic outreach principle: people tend to relate better and respond more positively to people with similar ethnic and social backgrounds. Taiwanese people will be more effective in reaching Taiwanese people. Mainland Chinese will be more effective in reaching Mainland Chinese. The challenge evangelistically is to put people of the same cultural and socioeconomic backgrounds together.

As a minister of outreach, Bob tries to create activities where he can bring together like people: students with students, professionals with professionals, college faculty with college faculty.

Another important concept Bob referred to was the idea of *people being willing to cross status boundaries to serve and lead the lost to Christ.* Some people are not comfortable with the fact that American society is stratified

113

into class and status groupings. Comfortable or not, it is a reality. It's not wrong; it's just the way things are. All complex societies are stratified by class and status. Doctors have a higher social status than plumbers; college professors have a higher status than sales clerks. Those with a higher status must be willing to cross status boundaries to serve those who do not share their social status. The humility involved in this kind of service can impact the recipients of such kindness in powerful ways, creating teaching and discipling opportunities.

When asked, what ministry or nurturing methods work best with Chinese believers, Bob spoke of *the importance of nurturing new believers in a one-on-one personal context.* Bob has 12 to 15 mature believers trained to work with new believers in a personal discipling relationship. They use an eight-lesson series of study material for new believers designed to teach the basics about Christianity. A "Christianity 101" new convert's class at church is not enough. New believers need personal attention. They need to be taught, encouraged, and assimilated into the faith community in the context of a personal relationship with a mature believer.

Bob calls the material he uses FUN—follow-up nurturing. A FUN teacher might meet with a new convert an hour each week, taking two weeks to complete one of the eight lessons. Over the 16 weeks, new believers pray and study with their teachers, enjoy fellowships and find a place in the church to serve and be involved. Fellowship and involvement are the keys. It is not enough to provide opportunities and invite new believers to come and get involved. Most won't do that. There needs to be a personal relationship where someone who cares, who takes time to call and invite and encourage, or to go by and pick up the new believer, making sure he or she is present and involved.

Advice: When asked, what advice would he give church leaders who want to work effectively with immigrants, Bob said there were several factors he believed were crucial:

1. leaders need to evaluate the church. Who in the church is already ministering to immigrants? Who is available for such a ministry? How ready is the church for such an undertaking?

2. the church needs to be prepared spiritually to reach out and serve those who are new to this country. Spiritual formation must precede outreach.

3. leaders need to evaluate the community. What cultural groups are present? What sub-cultural groups are present? In what percentages are they present? What are the differences between the groups. What are similarities? Are they separate outreach groups or can they be reached in a single effort? Leaders need to know and understand the community they are called to serve.

4. outreach needs to be truly relevant. The needs of a specific group must be met in ways that resonate with that group. The needs of one immigrant group may not be the same as the needs of another. The needs of immigrants from China are not the same as the needs of immigrants from Mexico. And the needs of Chinese from Taiwan are not identical to those of the Chinese from mainland China. For our outreach to be relevant, we must understand the people of our communities.

4. Background: Tino is from Mexico. He came to the U.S. in 1982 when he was thirteen. Tino's father was a U.S. citizen, a third generation American. Tino's mother was a first generation immigrant. They met in Chicago. Tino's mother preferred living in Mexico so eventually she and the children moved back to Mexico. Tino's father sent money to them in Mexico where they lived well. But the family needed to be together so when Tino was thirteen the family was reunited in Texas.

115

Tino's family was Catholic but, as is the case with many good Catholic families, they lacked the skills to apply theology to daily life. Tino got married right after high school and all the extended family lived near each other in Texas. Tino's wife's younger sisters were riding a "Joy Bus" to a local church, attending VBS and Sunday school. They were enjoying it. Tino's wife wanted to go with her younger sisters and see what they were doing. She did and found it interesting and helpful. In a few weeks she convinced Tino to come with her. In time Tino was converted and got involved. His casual involvement became serious involvement and eventually he decided that he wanted to be a minister. In 1995 he and his family moved to Dallas so he could complete a ministry training program. Tino has been involved in ministry to Latinos for nine years.

Ministry Insights: When asked, what is the most challenging aspect of ministry to Latinos, Tino said that *since most of the Latinos [in his congregation] are young there is not a lot of leadership available.* Of course, congregational demographics change from church to church, but a lack of mature, willing leaders is often a challenge in Latino churches.

Another challenge Tino explained, especially for Mexicans, is *a lack of confidence that grows out of their cultural history.* Since the Conquistadors arrived in this part of the world in the 1500s, conquering, pillaging, and mating with as many Aztec women as possible (thus creating a hybrid European-Indian people known as Mexicans), Mexico has been a nation of conquered, oppressed people. Their rulers were interested in controlling a subservient people, not producing a society of educated, motivated people. Four hundred years of that kind of treatment tends to take its toll on a people's identity and self-image.

When asked, *what outreach method is most effective in working with Latinos,* Tino said, *I know definitely what does not work—a theological presentation about doctrinal differences. What works is a focus on practical, family issues.* A few years ago, Tino participated in a community-wide research project sponsored by church and educational leaders. The research was designed to discover community feelings about how well local churches and schools were meeting family needs. The majority of respondents felt that local churches were providing enough "religion." However, families felt that what they were not getting from local churches was help with practical, family oriented matters. They needed and wanted help with issues of daily living. They wanted to live better lives. They didn't feel the church was very helpful with that.

Tino's point is that effective outreach has to meet people's perceived needs. (This is the same point Bob—in the previous section—was making). If people feel that they need help with family issues, then the church needs to offer help with family issues. If a church finds itself in a "family" community, that church needs to offer counseling, seminars, activities and programs designed to meet family needs. In Tino's context, an outreach orientation that is focused on the family is what works.

Of course, all outreach, Tino acknowledges, must be accomplished in the larger context of relationship and friendship. People need to know and trust one another before teaching and influence and change can occur. Relationship is the foundation for all effective outreach.

When asked, what methods of nurturing and ministry are effective in working with Latinos, Tino explained that *there must be an emphasis on community. The church "family" must eat together, enjoying each other's company, being part of each other's lives. In that kind of intimate community, teaching and growth can occur.*
Advice: When asked, what advice do you have for church leaders who want to work effectively with immigrants, Tino offered a list of four things.

117

1. *Church leaders need to determine who, exactly, they want to reach. Which ethnic group do they have in mind?* Tino's answer implies several factors. Church leaders need to do some research. Part of understanding who they want to reach includes understanding that people's culture, the way they think, their values, the way their society works.

2. *Hire a minister from that ethnic group and begin researching specific needs. Using a community survey, for instance, may reveal some specific social concerns among that ethnic group.*

3. *Go slow. Give the minister between six to twelve months before he attempts to start a church. Give him time to work in the community, to make contacts, to build relationships, to build bridges of service and communication.*

4. *During those six to twelve months, formulate a plan based on what is being learned about the community. Spend time serving and working in the community before attempting to start a church. Use the time to build relationships.*

In overview, Tino explained that church leaders must avoid setting unrealistic goals. They need to slow down and give outreach to a specific ethnic group time to work. Outreach to non-Western people (which is what most immigrants are) is rooted in relationship. Relationships take time to develop. So slow down and let it work. Don't expect much to happen in the first year.

5. Background: Sovanna is from Cambodia. Sovanna came to the U.S. in 1981 when he was 22. When the communists took over the country Sovanna was put into a camp where he lived for three years. He met and married his wife during those years. Sovanna was a Buddhist, as were his wife and her sisters. There were some Christians in the camp and Sovanna used to make fun of them. But he was curious about what they believed. One day he went to the place where they met. No one was there, but Sovanna saw a Cambodian Bible someone had left behind. He took it and began reading. That was his introduction to Christianity—a stolen Bible.

When Sovanna and his family got a sponsor so they could enter the U.S., they were eager to begin a new life. Their sponsor, a minister, gave them an English Bible and helped with many things. This impressed Sovanna. In less than one year he became a Christian. As Sovanna's English skills improved he was invited to translate from English into Cambodian for a minister who was working with Cambodian immigrants. Without realizing it, Sovanna was learning how to preach. Before long he was preaching to the Cambodian immigrants. Sovanna has been in ministry 23 years now. He still has the Cambodian Bible he stole that day.

Ministry Insights: When asked, what is the most challenging aspect of ministry to Cambodians, Sovanna explained that *most Cambodians are so deeply rooted in Buddhism that getting them to consider Christianity is difficult. This is especially true for older Cambodians who are set in their cultural ways. A different way of thinking about how to live life* (which is what Christianity offers) *is not appealing.*

When asked, what methods of outreach are effective in working with Cambodians, Sovanna explained (as did Tino) that *a direct confrontational approach (if you were to die tonight are you sure you would go to heaven?) does not work.* For a Buddhist, that question doesn't even make sense. Like so many others, Sovanna, says what works best is to develop a relationship with someone and in time begin talking with them about spiritual matters. People from other cultures are simply not willing to open up and discuss important matters of heart, family and cultural identity with people they do not know and trust. Time is one of the crucial factors in effective outreach to immigrants. Another is a willingness to help. Give them the help they need. Let them see God's love.

When asked, what methods of nurturing and ministry work best with Cambodians, Sovanna explained that *there must be lots of fellowship. There must be time to eat together, to share life. Then, in Bible classes there can be questions and interaction that will allow people to think and learn.*

Advice: When asked, what advice do you have for church leaders who want to reach out to immigrants? Sovanna noted three things.

1. *Church leaders must understand that immigrants are shy. They will not assert themselves and join in. They need to be invited. They need to be made to feel welcome. It must be clear to them that this whole group of people value their presence and participation. If they need help, give it to them.*

2. *The more people in the church that are involved with the immigrants the better. Immigrants need to feel welcomed by all not just a few.*

3. *Immigrants must be assisted in their integration into the church so that they feel like members of a large extended family.* The church must be presented (by Anglos) and perceived (by the immigrants) as a family. It is that family orientation that will attract them and keep them connected.

6. Background: Oscar is from Colombia. He came to the U.S. in 1978 when he was 19 to go to college in Florida. He stayed until 1982 when he returned to Colombia. During his time in Florida, Oscar was converted from Catholicism to a conservative protestant expression of the Christian faith. In Colombia, Oscar was active in a local church.

Oscar's family was part of the upper middle class and when missionaries came to his city to work there they wanted to reach the middle class. It was difficult and not many people responded. Oscar observed all this, believing the missionaries were right in what they wanted to accomplish, but realizing their failure and frustration were inevitable. Oscar wondered if there were methods that would allow them to accomplish their purpose.

Oscar had a friend in another city who was a minister and who gave Oscar's name to a recruiter from a small ministry training school in America. The recruiter contacted Oscar to offer him a scholarship if he was interested in training for ministry. Oscar remembered the missionaries. Some of Oscar's family lived in the U.S., so after thinking and discussing it with his wife for several days, Oscar accepted the offer and in 1993 came to the U.S. to train for the ministry. He has remained in the States working with Latinos. He has been in ministry now for 11 years.

Ministry Insights: When asked, what is the most challenging aspect of ministry to Latinos, Oscar explained that *when people from Latin America or Mexico come to the U.S., most do so for economic reasons. They want to make money and build a better life for themselves and their families. Consequently, when they get here they get a first job to pay the bills and then a second job so they will have the extra money it takes to build the better life they wanted. They work long hours and are tired at the end of the day. Any spare time they have is allocated for family and relaxation. Church is not high on their list of priorities.*

A second major challenge is changing the way people think—Latinos and Anglos. Most Anglos seem to think that the way they do church is the way church ought to (must) be done. When they decide to start outreach to a specific group they simply assume that the new group will meet and do things basically the way the Anglos do, except in their own language.

Most Anglo leaders fail to consider that their structures and patterns for the church may not be effective for another cultural group. So (from Oscar's perspective) there is the struggle of trying to educate the Anglo leaders regarding church forms and structures, while trying to integrate Latinos into a way of thinking about and doing church that is foreign to them.

The "ethnic minister" is often stuck in the middle between Anglo leaders who do not understand (and who do not realize that they do not understand) and newly converted immigrants who also do not understand why things are the way they are. Stuck in the middle is never a comfortable place to be.

When asked, *what outreach method is most effective in working with Latino immigrants,* Oscar explained that *a family orientation is a must. There must be a group of families that make up the core of the church. Those families need to agree on objectives and work well together. They need to approach local North American ministry as if they were in a foreign field. They need to see themselves as a missions/ministry team sent to a location to plant and nurture the church.*

Once this team is in place, they should use a number of outreach tools: ESL, immigration information and services, seminars on culture, the legal system, the educational system, the medical system, family issues and so forth—subjects immigrants need help with. The team needs to be of service to the community, making contacts, building relationships. Then there will be opportunities to teach.

When asked, what methods of nurturing and ministry are effective with Latinos, Oscar said that *getting people involved was the key. To be involved, however, they need to be taught. So there must be classes on the basics of the Christian faith and life.* As people begin to grow they must be involved, active, busy.

Another important aspect of nurturing is maintaining an emphasis on the family. The family is the central focus of Latino life. The church must be a group of families that becomes a large extended family.

Finally, the church must find a way to meet people's emotional needs. Some [Anglo] churches are so rationalistic that there is little in the way of emotional appeal. Yet Latinos are emotional people. If a church family is going to appeal to Latinos, it must address their emotional needs. Churches do not need to be Pentecostal or Charismatic to do this. But they do need to understand that people are both rational and emotive and faith must touch the heart as much as it touches the mind.

Advice: When asked, what advice do you have for church leaders who want to engage in effective outreach to immigrants, Oscar noted five things he felt were important.

1. *It's going to take money.* Even if the new church is going to meet in the Anglo church's facilities, thus avoiding the expense of a building, planting a new church is an expensive proposition. Adequate resources need to be allocated. How much adds up to "adequate" will depend on many factors and no one other than a local leadership in a given community context can determine the final amount. But a shoestring budget is probably not a good idea. If the planting has to be delayed a year or two until adequate funds are available, there is important work that can be done in the meantime.

2. *Leaders should consider using a team approach. One individual cannot plant a church by himself.* Oscar has made an important point here. Earlier he noted that we should think of local North American outreach as mission work. We should design and implement local outreach in North America just the way we would if we were planning a foreign mission work. To plant a church (even if it is in connection with an existing Anglo church), Oscar suggests, requires more than one individual. A team of families can be more effective than one person can ever hope to be. Utilizing a team approach costs more and takes longer to prepare for, but in the long run it may produce a stronger, healthier church.

3. *Leaders must learn and understand the culture and language of the people they want to reach.* Take the time to

learn the language. In learning the language you learn a great deal of the culture.

4. *Leaders (and Anglos in general) need to understand that they can learn something from the immigrants to whom they are reaching out.* Because the immigrants may not yet know the Lord does not mean that they know nothing! Most of them come from cultures older than our American culture and they have rich and useful insights on how to live and what is important. We can learn from them.

5. *Finally, leaders need to understand that planting a new church among a given ethnic group is not a church program. It is not something to be undertaken on a "probationary" basis—"let's give it a try and see how it works."* The church of Jesus among a group of people is not a program. It is spiritual life or death. It is eternity.

Summary

In this summary, I will simply list the advice each of the ministers had for church leaders. There will be some repetition, but I believe it will be helpful.

1. Leaders need to devote plenty of time to learning and understanding the cultural group they are interested in working with.

2. Leaders need to communicate with and get a commitment from the whole church to be involved in and dedicated to the challenge of being a multiethnic church.

3. Leaders need to be open to learning from the new cultural group.

4. The most important thing is to create within the whole church an atmosphere where Anglos and non-Anglos can interact safely, without the fear of compromising their ethnic identity. There can be no cultural domination. People must be allowed to be who they are—culturally speaking.

5. Leaders need to evaluate the church. Who in the church is already ministering to immigrants? Who is available for such a ministry? How ready is the church for such an undertaking?

6. The church needs to be prepared spiritually to reach out and serve those who are new to this country. Spiritual formation must precede outreach.

7. Leaders need to evaluate the community. What cultural groups are present? What sub-cultural groups are present? In what percentages are they present? What are the differences between the groups? What are similarities? Are they separate outreach groups or can they be reached in a single effort? Leaders need to know and understand the community they are called to serve.

8. Outreach needs to be truly relevant. The needs of a specific group must be met in ways that resonate with that group. The needs of one immigrant group may not the same as the needs of another. The needs of immigrants from China are not the same as the needs of immigrants from Mexico. And the needs of Chinese from Taiwan are not identical to those of the Chinese from mainland China. For our outreach to be relevant, we must understand the people of our communities.

9. Church leaders need to determine who, exactly, they want to reach. Which ethnic group do they have in mind?

10. Hire a minister from that ethnic group and begin researching specific needs. Using a community survey, for instance, may reveal some specific social concerns among that ethnic group.

11. Go slow. Give the minister between six to twelve monthsto work in the community, to make contacts, to build relationships, to build bridges of service and communication before he attempts to start a church.

12. During those six to twelve months formulate a plan based on what is being learned about the community. Spend time

serving and working in the community before attempting to start a church. Use the time to build relationships.

13. Church leaders must understand that immigrants are shy. They will not assert themselves and join in. They need to be invited. They need to be made to feel welcome. It must be clear to them that this whole group of people value their presence and participation. If they need help, give it to them.

14. The more people in the church that are involved with the immigrants the better. Immigrants need to feel welcomed by all, not just a few.

15. Immigrants must be assisted in their integration into the church so that they feel like members of a large extended family. The church must be presented [by Anglos] and perceived [by the immigrants] as a family. It is that family orientation that will attract them and keep them connected.

16. Its going to take money.

17. Leaders should consider using a team approach. One individual cannot plant a church by himself.

18. Leaders must learn and understand the culture and language of the people they want to reach. Take the time to learn the language.

19. Leaders (and Anglos in general) need to understand that they can learn something from the immigrants to whom they are reaching out.

20. Finally, leaders need to understand that planting a new church among a given ethnic group is not a church program. It is not something to be undertaken on a "probationary" basis—"let's give it a try and see how it works." The church of Jesus among a group of people is not a program.

This is good advice that church leaders need to keep in mind as they consider planting an ethnic church. In the next chapter we will discuss some of the background work that is necessary to successful ethnic church planting.

Chapter 6

Planting Ethnic Churches

Strictly speaking, all churches are ethnic churches because all people belong to an ethnic group. The term *ethnically-other* churches might be more accurate but it is cumbersome and perhaps overly technical. So let us speak in terms of *ethnic churches* and understand that we are referring to churches made up of people from ethnic groups that do not represent the majority or dominant population group of a given society. The dominant population group in the U.S. is "white." I prefer the term Anglos, even though many white people are not actually of Anglo-Saxon ethnicity. In the context of this study then, churches that are not predominantly Anglo churches are ethnic churches, whether they are Black, Latino, Chinese, African, Indian, Korean, Pakistani, Cambodian or any other cultural or sub-cultural group.

An ethnic church is not necessarily a church made up of recent or not so recent immigrants. An ethnic church might be made up of second or third or twenty-fifth generation Americans who prefer to retain a sub-cultural ethnic identity rather than be assimilated into mainstream Anglo culture.

How, then, does a church go about establishing (*planting*) a church that is designed to meet the spiritual needs of a specific cultural group? This chapter will provide a basic survey of some of the major considerations of ethnic church planting.

Studying Your Community

There is no substitute for detailed, factual information. Anyone can drive through sections of town and see that things are changing. Things look and feel different. Because we are followers of Jesus, a kind, compassionate response wells up in our hearts. But for our resources to be allocated in meaningful ways our response to community change and need must be carefully considered, designed, and implemented. The first step in that careful consideration is specific, detailed research into the demographics of your community.

To illustrate what I'm talking about I have chosen a Texas community that is a suburb of Dallas. Irving, Texas is a community of approximately 195,000 people (in July 2004). There are nearly 98,000 males and 94,000 females. The median age (in 2000) was 30 years old (a young community) with an average household income of nearly $45,000. The average house value (again in 2000) was $94,000.

The ethnic breakdown of Irving is as follows:

White non-Hispanic (Anglos) 48.2%
Hispanic 31.2%
Other races 13.4%
Black 10.2%
Asian Indian 3.3%
Two or more races 3.2%
Korean 1.3%
Other Asian 1.2%

American Indian 1.2%
Vietnamese 0.9%
Chinese 0.8% (Irving, Texas, Detailed Profile 2006)

Obviously there is a significant Latino presence in Irving. Knowing the exact percentages is important. But other information is just as important. On the *city-data* website (http://www.city-data.com), a website that provides detailed community demographic information nationwide, one can also find information regarding educational levels, marriage and family information, immigration information (specifically, the percentage of the population that are foreign-born), how many people commute out of the city to work, crime statistics (which have to do with living conditions), medical and educational institutions, and other helpful information, including an analysis of the demographics compared to other cities in the state.

How is this kind of information helpful? One can drive through the city and see that there are lots of Latinos. Why are the detailed demographics important? Because the demographics provide insights into the makeup of the community (and the needs of the community) where the church will be planted. For instance, in Irving, the median age is less than in the rest of the state—30.3 years. The unemployment rate is at or lower than the national average and the average commute to work is 24 minutes. The foreign-born population in Irving is higher than in the rest of the state. The percentage of people renting as opposed to buying their homes is also higher, and the length of time between moves is shorter. Over 51% are married, over 14% are divorced or separated.

On another website, the Irving Independent School District, one can easily find information regarding bilingual and immigrant students. Irving has 10,500 bi-lingual or ESL students that represent 80 different languages spoken in that school district (www.irvingisd.net/bilingual-esl 2006).

What this adds up to for Irving is a population that is significantly Latino, most of whom are younger, many are married with children (or single parents with children) and employed. It is likely, then, that a church plant in that community will result in a church of younger families with children.

From this, three factors emerge: 1) outreach into such a community should be geared to young families with children, 2) the ministry focus within the church must also be geared to young families with children, and 3) the individual (or individuals—assuming the possibility of a team approach) called to this kind of ministry should probably be younger people with children.

Outreach into a community such as Irving, and ministry within a church in that community must be focused on matters such as child care, health care, education, parenting, building strong marriages and healthy families, finances, adult continuing education, careers options and so forth.

Driving through a community may give one an overall sense that things have changed and that something needs to be done, but it is studying the details of local demographics that help clarify specific needs and potential outreach and ministry foci.

Hiring an Ethnically Compatible, Appropriately Educated Church Planter

Hiring the right person for the job is one of the most crucial factors in the success of any undertaking. Hiring the wrong person can be disastrous. Finding the right person can be a long and challenging process. In this section, I want to suggest two factors that are crucial in hiring the right person: ethnicity and education. This is not to say that ethnicity and education are the only important factors. Certainly they are not. But they are two basic considerations that are extremely important in ethnic church planting.

First, ethnicity is important because no one can reach a given ethnic group like a person from that ethnic group. Missionaries learned this a long time ago. It is important to learn a people's language. An Anglo who learns Spanish or Mandarin, or Portuguese, may enjoy some success in reaching out to people who speak those languages. But he or she will never be as successful reaching people of those ethnic groups as someone who is himself or herself one of those people. So if you want to plant an ethnic church, hire a person who is of the ethnic group you want to evangelize.

This broad categorization, however, is only a place to begin. As we learned from Bob, Chinese from Mainland China and Chinese from Taiwan are not the same. They are distinct sub-cultural groups. If you live in a community where there is a significant population of immigrants from Mainland China, you would not want to hire someone from Taiwan if there was a viable candidate available from Mainland China. If you were considering planting a church in a community such as Irving, with a significant population of immigrants from El Salvador (and wanted to specifically target that ethnic group), a minister from Mexico might not be the best choice, even though he speaks the same language as people from El Salvador. The cultures of Mexico and El Salvador are completely different. In that case, if it is possible, you should look for someone from El Salvador.

If, however, you live in a community with a growing Latino population from a number of Latino cultures (there are 22 separate Latino cultures), then hiring a person from a specific Latino cultural group may not be as crucial.

Second, education becomes an important factor because effective church planting requires some specialized training and not all schools that educate ministers offer extensive training in church planting. A number of ministry education programs, whether in Bible colleges, Christian universities or theological seminaries (at least those associated with conservative Christianity) approach the education of ministers with a greater emphasis placed on theology than on other more practical (people-oriented) ministry subjects. While theology and biblical studies are important components of ministry education, they should not be given greater weight than other ministry components. Given the missional nature of the church and her role in the world—to participate with God in his mission in the world, which is the reconciliation of all lost people (Rogers 2002)— ministry must be understood missiologically. Ministers are missionaries. At least they are supposed to be. But many are not mission-oriented because they were educated with a theological "church maintenance" orientation rather than a missiological "missions" orientation.

People are not saved nor do churches grow because of or based on theological presentations. Relationships, not theology, provide the foundation for missions and spiritual formation. Preaching the Gospel and helping people grow spiritually involves theology. Theology is essential. But in biblical ministry that is appropriately rooted in missions, theology and biblical studies are only part of the equation and should not be the primary concern.

I have said all that to say this: when looking for an appropriate person to plant an ethnic church, there is more to look for than someone who has an education in Bible, theology or even "Ministry." Church planting is a specialized endeavor that requires special training. A minister may be a fine theologian and not be an effective church planter because he lacks the specialized education necessary to plant and nurture a new church.

So what should church leaders look for "educationally" when searching for a person to plant a new church? An individual who has missions training or specific church planting training is the ideal candidate. There are a number of schools that offer degrees in missions. Others offer various ministry degrees with an emphasis in church planting. The more training and fieldwork an individual has in church planting the better. If you want to plant a church, look for someone who has been specifically educated in church planting.

This does not mean that someone who has not had specific training in church planting or missions can't do a fine job. There are missionaries and church planters who have a traditional theologically oriented education who have planted and nurtured growing churches around the world. I'm simply suggesting that we increase our chances for success if we work with people who have specialized training in what we are trying to accomplish.

What about socioeconomic and status compatibility? This may not be a major point, but it is worth mentioning. During our research, one of converts we interviewed spoke of the importance of socioeconomic-educational (status) compatibility. He did not use those words but that is what he was talking about. He was a Mexican immigrant with a ninth grade education. In Mexico, education is mandatory only through the ninth grade. That's why many Mexican immigrants have only a ninth grade education. This gentleman spoke of the importance of having ministers who are "like" the people they are trying to reach—someone who understands what it is like to be a laborer-class immigrant. To hire a second generation college educated Latino to reach first generation Mexican immigrant laborers may not be the best situation. Again, this is not to say that an educated second generation Latino can't do the work effectively in that context. But it may suggest that he will have to work very hard to understand the ministry context in which he is working.

Community and Church Resources: What's Available and What's Not—Discovering a Need and Meeting It

Once a church has an ethnically compatible and appropriately educated church planter on board, one of the first things he will want to do is discover what kind of resources exist within the community that are designed to benefit the ethnic group the church wants to reach.

The needs of immigrants can be dramatically different, depending on where they migrate from and why. For instance, immigrants from China often arrive with financial resources and are enrolled in a graduate program. They may not need financial help, but they will need help with the language and culture. They will need to build relationships with people, making friends who can become their family in this new place. Immigrants who arrive from Mexico will usually have very different goals and circumstances. They may have some needs that immigrants from China will not have. But nearly all immigrants, regardless of where they are from, will need help with the language and the culture. And they will value friendship.

Nearly all communities will have some resources in place to meet some of the needs of immigrants. Some of these resources will be federal, state or local government sponsored resources. Others will be available through educational institutions (student associations that assist foreign students in various ways), or local churches that are providing different forms of assistance to immigrants. Church leaders need to discover what kinds of assistance is already available to the people they want to reach.

The internet is a good place to begin looking for available resources. For instance, the State of Utah has an Office of Ethnic Affairs. Their website[2] lists a great deal of useful information including a second address for local

---

[2] http://ethnicoffice.utah.gov/communityresources.html

community resources[3]. Most states and local communities will have some resources available. Being able to direct immigrants to available resources is an important service.

Local churches may offer a number of resources to immigrants. These may include English and culture classes, various kinds of benevolence assistance, student fellowships, youth activities, informational seminars, child care and more.

Once church leaders know what resources are already available in the community, they can determine what needs are not being met, or not met thoroughly, and design programs to meet those needs. If, for example, a given community seems to have sufficient resources for learning English and for legal assistance, job training and placement, and after school youth programs, but there appears to be little directed toward family developmental concerns for young parents, that is a need that is not being adequately met.

One of the complaints some immigrant parents have, many of whom are from more conservative, traditional societies, has to do with the impact of our morally lax American society on their children. Church leaders might develop a seminar (in Spanish) called *The Challenges of American Society for the Latino Family*. It could be a two hour community seminar presented in the evening at a local school auditorium. This would not be a church service and sermon, but a community interest seminar offering suggestions on developing strong, healthy families. Christians need to be present, interacting with parents, but not pushing the church. The point is to make contacts and begin building relationships.

A little research into the community will reveal what resources are already available to immigrants, and what needs are not being adequately met. With a little creative thinking, those needs can be met, opening doors into a

---

[3] www.utahcares.utah.gov

community of people where relationships can be built, trust established, and lives eventually changed.

Preparing The Anglo Congregation

One of the biggest challenges in preparing to plant an ethnic church is educating and preparing the Anglo church for full support and participation in the process. People are naturally ethnocentric, that is, their thinking is rooted in their own ethnic perspective, believing their ways of thinking and behaving are the right and proper ways of thinking and behaving. It is normal for people to think this way. The African bushman is just as ethnocentric as the American businessman, who is just as ethnocentric as the Chinese farmer, who is just as ethnocentric as the Indian merchant, who is just as ethnocentric as the Latino housewife. However, because a thing occurs naturally does not mean it is something to be proud of. Ethnocentrism needs to be understood, monitored and minimized as much as is humanly possible.

Christians need to understand that God loves cultural variation. His world would be a very dull place if everyone thought and acted alike. We need to learn to appreciate different ways of communicating, different ways of thinking about life, about what's important, about priorities and values, about family, work, relationships, time and a dozen other things that impact our lives on a daily basis. Christians need to learn that their way of thinking about anything is only one way of thinking about that thing. Christians need to learn that perspective is everything, that if they lived life in a different place they would think about life very differently. All people are creatures of their culture. We think our faith has formed us. But whatever formation our faith has provided has occurred within the context of our specific culture. We are not merely Christians. We are Anglo-American Christians. Our perspective may be Christian, but it is also Anglo-American. It is impossible for Christianity to exist absent some cultural context. Christianity in America is American Christianity.

Once Anglos begin to understand that their way of thinking about things represents one possible way of thinking about things, and that other peoples have other ways of thinking that are just as valid as our ways, then they are ready to begin thinking of immigrants as equals who are simply looking for a better life. This is crucial. For a church to successfully plant an ethnic church, Anglos must think of the ethnic group involved as equals who have something to offer. They have to see them as people with whom they could be friends, people with whom they could enjoy a relationship.

Until most of the members of the existing church learn to think of immigrants as equals with whom they could enjoy a relationship, as people with a rich cultural heritage who have something to offer, the existing church is not ready to plant an ethnic church. Teaching believers the details of what to do and how to do it in a cross-cultural church planting context is the easy part. For the most part those are surface-level behaviors that can be learned. The hard part of preparing an existing church for a cross-cultural church planting experience involves the deep-level, underlying thinking and assumptions people have about themselves and others. Addressing those deep-level issues is a challenge that takes time and patience.

Summary

When church leaders begin thinking about planting an ethnic church they need to pause and spend the time and effort to do a community analysis. Demographic information is available on line for just about every community in the nation. The more church leaders know about their community the better prepared they are to make the kinds of decisions that go along with planting an ethnic church.

Once leaders understand their community and some of the needs that exist, if planting an ethnic church seems to be where the Lord is leading them, then the next step is to locate an ethnically compatible, appropriately educated church planter. Ethnic compatibility involves more than language. For instance, there are 22 Latino cultures. Each of them shares a common language—Spanish, but their cultures are very different. If your community has a significant number of people that belong to a specific cultural group, church leaders should think in terms of finding a church planter who is of that culture.

Also, Church leaders should think in terms of finding someone with specific church planting education. Church planting is a specialized endeavor that is enhanced by familiarity with specific methodologies. An individual with an education that is specifically related to missions or church planting has a greater likelihood of being successful.

Once an appropriate person to lead the planting effort has been found, he should busy himself with discovering what kinds of resources are available to immigrants. What services are government agencies offering? Are charitable agencies or educational institutions offering helpful services? What are local churches doing? Once church leaders are aware of community needs and the kinds of resources that are already available, they can formulate a plan to meet the needs that are not currently being met.

Finally, in preparing to plant an ethnic church the Anglo church must be prepared to support and participate in the new church plant. The primary concern that needs to be addressed has to do with the deep-level, underlying assumptions the Anglos have about themselves and about immigrants. Ethnocentricism needs to be monitored and minimized. Different cultural ways does not add up to inferior cultural ways. Less money does not add up to inferior. Less education does not add up to inferior. Less technology does not add up to inferior. All people are created in God's image and all people are equal—even if they think and behave different than do Anglos. Until the Anglo church really believes this, outreach to immigrants will not work.

Chapter seven will explore the idea of the missional church as it exists in a multiethnic society.

Chapter 7

The Missional Church in a Multiethnic Society

In my book, *What in the World Does God Want: God's Purpose in Creation, God's Purpose for His Church*, I discuss the missional nature of the church, demonstrating that God's desire for a relationship with all people is the underlying metatheme of his communication to us in the Scriptures. His mission is the reconciliation of all people. That's why God became a human being in the person of Jesus and died to provide a sacrifice of atonement, so all people could be saved. The church's mission in the world is to participate with God in his mission of reconciliation. The very nature of the church is missional. Missions is what the church is about.

I'm not going to duplicate that material here. However, it may be helpful to think of the missional nature of the church in relation to the multiethnic nature of our society, and concerns regarding unity and diversity that grow out of missions that occur in a multiethnic context.

The Missional Multiethnic Church

When we speak of the missional nature of the church we mean that the church is, by nature, a missions institution. It is a group of saved people who are supposed to be busy telling the story of salvation to everyone that will listen, so as many people as possible can be reconciled to God and saved. Saved people are supposed to save other people. The church is about missions. The church is missional in nature.

The world is multiethnic. There are thousands of different ethnic groups throughout the world. People from nearly all those ethnic groups live among us, so our American society is multiethnic. A reality that needs to be faced, however, is that our society is more ethnically diverse than the Lord's church in America. We're not keeping up. We need to think more clearly about our presence in society. We need to think more clearly about *the missional church in a multiethnic society*. How can the two realities come together in each local church so that each church can be a missional, multiethnic church?

The Missional Multiethnic Church is Intentionally Missional in Orientation

Outreach does not occur by accident. The church doesn't come to understand who and what it is by accident. Important spiritual and theological concepts are not transmitted from one generation of Christians to another by some sort of spiritual osmosis. If the universal church is to be a missional church, then each local church must be a missional church. For that to happen, leaders in local churches must have an *intentional missions orientation*. Leaders must understand the missional nature of the church and must instill a missional orientation (a missional or missions way of thinking) in the church they lead. The whole church must think of itself as a missional church whose mission in the world is to participate with God in his mission—the reconciliation of all lost people. This doesn't happen unless the leaders of local churches have a very intentional missions orientation.

In their book, *The Status of Missions*, Gailyn Van Rheenen and Bob Waldron discuss the role of elders and preachers in the local church's thinking about missions. The key is to keep missions on the minds of the members. The more often preachers preach about mission the more the church thinks of itself as a mission oriented church (2002:22-25).

Having an intentional missions orientation means understanding the missional nature of the church. It means teaching believers about the missional nature of the church. It means talking about missions (from the pulpit on Sunday morning) often enough and passionately enough that the church thinks of itself as God's tool for accomplishing his mission in the world.

But having an intentional missions orientation also means that the church is structured in such a way that ministry within the body (nurturing and spiritual formation) is accomplished with a missions goal in mind. Everything the church does to nurture believers, to help them grow and mature into productive believers, must be intentionally missions oriented. The teaching that occurs in the church, the counseling, the discipling, all the ministry, all the programs within the church designed to help believers become the people God wants them to be must be focused on the end result: those believers going into the world to participate with God in his mission—the reconciliation of all lost people.

Being intentionally missional in orientation is not an easy thing. It has to do with foundational concepts of who and what we are as God's people, and what we are to be doing in his world. An intentional missional orientation impacts every aspect of who we are and what we do as the church.

The Missional Multiethnic Church is Intentionally Multiethnic in Implementation

Just as the church must be intentionally missional in orientation, it must also be intentionally multiethnic in implementation. Outreach to people who are *ethnically-other* doesn't happen by accident. It doesn't happen easily either. People prefer to be around other people who are like themselves. People from other ethnic groups are not like us. They do not think like we think. Their worldview is different. Their values are different. Their language is often different. The way they think about family, work, time, relationships, and a dozen other things is different. There are lots of differences and the differences sometimes make us so uncomfortable that we avoid the people so we don't have to deal with the differences.

But a missional church in a multiethnic society will be a multiethnic church. There's no way around it. So comfortable or not, we need to get past the differences and do (implement) what needs to be done so we can be the multiethnic church we need to be, the multiethnic church God wants us to be.

Being intentionally multiethnic in implementation requires that we design and implement strategies and processes that will facilitate effective communication and ministry across the ethnic boundaries that divide us. As we develop a missional orientation we must implement outreach strategies that will be effective in our multiethnic society. We must find ways to serve ethnic communities so they will come to know the love and grace of God. Only when we implement strategies for effective multiethnic outreach can we really claim to have a missional orientation. Even churches that are heavily engaged in foreign missions have failed to develop a truly intentional missional orientation if the foreign-born who live in their own community remain unchurched. For in a multiethnic society a missional church will be a multiethnic church.

The Missional Multiethnic Church is
Comfortable with a Diversified Unity

Some Christians seem to be under the impression that there is only one way to be a "biblical" multiethnic church. For them, everyone has to be in an ethnically integrated assembly. This is important, they insist, because of the need for unity. Support for their conclusion often includes references to the first-century church and an ethnically diverse Jew-Gentile context where Paul encouraged believers to be of one mind and spirit. The church at Ephesus, they believe, was one ethnically diverse but unified body of believers that met together in one integrated assembly. Their *perception* of unity in the apostolic church becomes a proof-text for their position—a unified church is one in which all believers worship in the same assembly.

There are two problems with this position. First, is the logic that unity demands integration. Is it necessary for believers to worship in the same assembly before they can enjoy the unity Jesus prayed for? No, it is not. Most large cities have multiple congregations of a given Christian fellowship meeting in that city. The Lord's church on Fourth Street and the Lord's church on Tenth Street can meet separately and still enjoy a unity of faith and purpose as local churches that are part of a given Christian fellowship and part of the one universal church but that meet in separate assemblies in separate locations.

Second, there is no reason to believe that all of the believers in Ephesus met in one big assembly. First-century believers met for worship in small groups in homes. The church in Ephesus (or Philippi, or Corinth, or Rome) was comprised of a number of house churches. It is unlikely that there were very many assemblies where all the believers in a city met together in one large group. This is not to suggest that there was no interaction between Jewish and non-Jewish believers. Of course there was. But the concept of a single congregation in Ephesus where everyone met together in one big assembly is without historical support.

The unity that Jesus prayed for and that Paul encouraged in the first-century was not a unity rooted in the surface-level uniformity of a single integrated worship assembly. Jesus was not terribly interested in anything that had to do with surface-level concerns. The unity Jesus longed for was a deep-level unity of spirit, relationship, purpose, and hope that would bind his followers together even when they were separated by surface-level factors such as language and culture.

Should Christians of different ethnic backgrounds be able to worship together? Certainly. And many foreign-born believers who have achieved a level of cultural assimilation that allows them to participate comfortably and meaningfully in an Anglo assembly do so happily. But not all foreign-born believers (perhaps not even most foreign-born believers) have achieved a level of cultural assimilation that allows for meaningful worship in an Anglo context.

Must Christians of different ethnic backgrounds worship in the same assembly before unity is possible? No. If different ethnic groups are worshiping separately because they don't like each other or can't get along, then there is a problem. But it should not be assumed that ethnic churches or worship assemblies exist because of (or that by their existence they create) a lack of unity.

Unity does not demand uniformity. Ethnic churches can be separate and "different" without sacrificing unity. A missional multiethnic church must learn to be comfortable with a diversified unity. We don't all have to be the same to be children of the same Father, servants of the same Lord, and members of the same church, sharing the same faith and spirit of purpose and hope.

Summary

The Lord's church is missional in nature. It is a body of reconciled people who are to participate with God in his mission in the world—the reconciliation of all people. Since the very nature of the church is missional, local churches must be intentional in their missions orientation. Our society is a multiethnic society. For the missional church to engage a multiethnic society it must be intentional in implementing strategies designed to penetrate and serve the various ethnic communities that exist in our cities. A missional church is a multiethnic church. And it is a church that is comfortable with the diversity of faith and worship expressions that grow out of ethnic diversity. Unity can exist without uniformity.

Conclusion

Immigration to the United States is providing the American church with one of the greatest evangelistic opportunities that has existed since the first century. The world is coming to America. For many, the journey to America is made in the face of daunting challenges. After arriving, the challenges continue in the form of acculturation, often without the resources that many of us would consider basic.

Most of us will never understand how hard it is to leave one's home culture and move to a new land with strange new customs. Most of us will never know how alone and overwhelmed a person in that situation can feel. But we can experience the joy of helping someone get through that difficult period of adjustment. Many of the people we interviewed spoke of the kindness of the Christians they met after arriving in the U.S. The acts of kindness those immigrants experienced impacted them in positive ways, opening their hearts to the story of Jesus.

Many of the people we interviewed explained a range of emotions and conditions that existed for them after their immigration. They explained that at some point after arriving in the U.S. they:

1. felt hurt, confused, empty or alone,
2. were experiencing personal or family illness or issues,

147

3. felt a need for God's presence in their lives,
4. felt a need to learn English and American culture,
5. felt the need for truth and spiritual guidance offered in the Bible,
6. felt a need for some clarity and understanding in their lives.

For the people we interviewed, and for tens of thousands of others, those emotions and conditions (needs) were met by Christians who were kind and caring and who made a difference in their lives. They told us about the kinds of life-changing things Christians did for them. Christians:

1. were loving, kind, friendly, and willing to help,
2. demonstrated Christianity by their actions,
3. did not push for a quick response, gave people time to watch, listen and learn,
4. made use of small group Bible studies and discussions,
5. provided teaching that was biblical in its source and content,
6. helped with physical needs—bills, food, transportation, housing, medical, and so forth,
7. invited them to church,
8. helped them focus on spiritual things and the value of God's presence in their lives,
9. offered programs for teaching English and American culture,
10. provided teaching that was relevant to life.
11. provided comfort and encouragement during times of difficulty,
12. invited them to fellowships and activities,
13. prayed for them,
14. developed a relationship with them,
15. spent time with them just being friends,
16. studied the Bible in their own language.

These ways of caring are marvelous examples of Christian love in action. They are the kinds of things that can be duplicated in every context by every church. The things immigrants said made a difference in their lives were not so much programs as they were people being kind and caring. That's the key: Christian love in action. *"By your love will all people know that you are my disciples."* Evidently Jesus knew what he was talking about.

Appendix A

**Religious Conversion Experiences of
First Generation Immigrants to America**

Interview Profile Data: Date:

First name or Pseudonym:

Country of Origin:

Gender:

Present Age:

Age when immigrated:

Year of Immigration:

Reason for immigration:

U.S. State immigrated to:

Educational level at time of immigration:

Current Educational Level:

Have you become, or are you in the process of becoming, an American citizen?

Religion before immigration:

Religion Converted to: Conservative Christian

How long after your immigration before your were converted?

What were the initial factors that prompted you to think about religion or spiritual matters? What got you started on your spiritual journey?

If you could speak to church leaders and advise them about how to work effectively with immigrants, what would you tell them?

Appendix B

Date:

Name

Country of origin

Year immigrated

Age when immigrated

Reason for immigration

Your conversion story

How long in ministry?

What ethnic group do you minister to?

What is the most challenging aspect of ministry to that group? Why

What is the most effective outreach method to that group? Why?

What is the most effective ministry/nurturing method to that group? Why?

What advice would you give to church leaders who want to begin a multiethnic church?

Works Cited

American Immigration
    2006   Reasons For Immigration
    http://www.bergen.org/AAST/porjects/Immigration/
    reasons_for_immigration.html

Barrett, David B, Todd M. Johnson, Peter F. Crossing.
    2006   Missiometrics 2006: Goals, Resources,
    Doctrines of the 350 Christian World Communions.
    International Bulletin of Missionary Research. 30
    (1) 28.

Center for Immigration Studies
    2006   Current Numbers.
    http://www.cis.org/topics/currentnumbers.html

Dallas Independent School district
    2006   *Inside DISD.*
    http://www.dallasisd.org/inside_disd/

Daniels, Roger
    2002   *Coming To America: A History of Immigration
    and Ethnicity in American Life.* Princeton: Perennial.

Delgado-Gaitan, Concha and Henry Trueba
    1991   *Crossing Cultural Borders: Education for
    Immigrant Families in America.* London: The
    Falmer Press.

Edaugh, Helen Rose and Janet Saltzman Chafetz
    2000   *Religion and the New Immigrants:
    Continuities and Adaptations in Immigrant
    Congregations.* Walnut Creek: Alta Mira Press.

Edmonston, Barry
    2006   Immigration Assumptions in Population
    Projections.http://www.ssab.gov/immigration-
    forum/documents/EDMONSTON.pdf

Hiebert, Paul G.
    1983   *Cultural Anthropology.* Grand Rapids: Baker.

Irving Independent School District
    2006   *Bilingual/ESL/Migrant Department.*
    http://www.irvingisd.net/bingual-
    esl/Menu/Countries_Represented.htm

Irving, Texas
    2006   *Irving, Texas.*
    http://www.city.data.com/city/Irving-Texas.html

Jenkins, Philip
    2002   *The Next Christendom: The Coming of Global
    Christianity.* Oxford University Press: Oxford.

Joselit, Jenna Weissman
    2001   *Immigration and American Religion.* Oxford:
    Oxford University Press.

Larsen, Luke J.
    2004   *The Foreign-Born Population in the United
    States: 2003.* Current Population Reports, P20-551,
    U.S. Census Bureau, Washington, D.C.

Meyers, Deborah and Jennifer Yau
    2004   *U.S. Immigration Statistics in 2003.*
    Migration Policy Institute.
    http://www.migrationinformation.org/Feature/print.cf
    m?ID=263

National Center for Policy Analysis
2002   *Rate of Immigration to the U.S. Highest in 150
Years.*
http://www.ncpa.org/iss/imm/2002/pd060502d.html

Passel, Jeffery S.
2005   *Unauthorized Migrants: Numbers and
Characteristics.* Washington, D.C.: Pew Hispanic
Center.

Portes, Alejandro and Ruben G. Rumbaut
1990   *Immigrant America: A Portrait.* Berkeley:
University of California Press.

Rogers, Glenn
2002   *What in the World Does God Want: God's
Purpose in Creation, God's Purpose for His Church.*
Bedford: Mission and Ministry Resources.

Siv, Sichan
2004   *Keynote Address: Dallas/Fort Worth Asian-
American Citizens Council.* Addison, TX.
http://www.un.int/usa/04ss0925.pdf

State of Utah
2006   *Office of Ethnic Affairs.*
http://ethnicoffice.utah.gov/communityresources.html

2006   *Utah Cares*
www.utahcares.utah.gov

Thompson, Richard
1996   Assimilation, in *Encyclopedia of Cultural
Anthropology.* David Levinson and Melvin Ember,
eds. New York: Henry Holt.

U.S. Census Bureau
  2002 *Coming To America: A Profile of the Nation's Foreign Born (2000 Update).* CENBR/01-1.

  2002 *Coming From the Americas: A Profile of the Nation's Foreign Born Population From Latin America (2000 Update).* CENBR/01-2.

  2002 *A Profile of the Nation's Foreign-Born Population From Asia (2000 Update).* CENBR/01-3.

  2440 U.S. Interim Projections by Age, Sex, Race, and Hispanic Origin.
  http://www.census.gov/ipc/www/usinterimproj/

U.S. Department of Homeland Security
  2006 *2004 Yearbook of Immigration Statistics.* U.S. Department of Homeland Security: Washington, D.C.

Van Rheenen, Gailyn and Bob Waldron
  2002 *The Status of Missions: A Nationwide Survey of Churches of Christ.* Abilene: ACU Press.

Wright, John W.
  2001 *The New York Times Almanac.* John Wright, ed. Penguin: New York.

CPSIA information can be obtained at www.ICGtesting.com
Printed in the USA
BVOW02s1624091013

333299BV00003B/587/A